Praise for the First Edition

Linda Ellen Perry has written from years of experience in guiding teens who found themselves pregnant before they were ready. Perry gives real-life advice to help parents work through all the issues they will face. The book is practical and Biblical, helping you work through things such as forgiveness, adoption possibilities, your teen parenting alone and what she needs from the adults in her life, welcoming a new baby into your home, and tons of resources. This is only a partial list for Perry has addressed every angle of the challenges faced when your daughter says those words, "Mom, Dad, I'm pregnant".
--T. Suzanne Eller, Author of "Real Teens, Real Stories, Real Life", and "Real Issues, Real Teens - What Every Parent Needs to Know". http://www.daretobelieve.org/

We picked this book up at a CPC retreat in Georgia. Reading it, I was very surprised and pleased at how it takes everyone's feelings into account. It goes step by step into emotions, choices, decisions, etc. The biblical aspect was very well done. I wish I could put several copies into each church in our community! Thank you.
--Meendy Couture, Co-Director, Pregnancy Helpline, Michigan

Linda Ellen Perry, an experienced pro-life activist and Executive Director of the Assist Crisis Pregnancy Center in Annandale, Virginia, is the author of How to Survive Your Teen's Pregnancy: Practical Advice for a Christian Family. Her 190-page paperback is a valuable resource for parents and daughter. It is designed as a step-by step guide and a workbook to help them face each problem in sequence, with appropriate, comforting scripture and spiritual advice. Real life stories based on Mrs. Perry's 12 years of pregnancy center counseling experience are woven into the text and provide encouragement and hope that lives can be changed in a powerful way.
--Eagle Forum News and Notes, September 27, 2002

When I first came to work at NOEL, one of the first concerns that came to my attention was the need of a Christian family seeking help in dealing with their teenage daughter's unplanned pregnancy. I remember feeling inadequate in trying to help because I had no experience or knowledge to draw from. And I couldn't find any resources to recommend. Well imagine my surprise a few weeks ago, when a book entitled How To Survive Your Teen's Pregnancy: Practical Advice for a Christian Family by Linda Ellen Perry arrived for NOEL to review!

The book is written as a devotional workbook with 33 short concise chapters. Each chapter addresses an issue to discuss, a decision to examine or an action that needs to be taken. In addition, every chapter recommends a related portion of Scripture, has real-life stories from others who survived their teen's pregnancy, journaling exercises, and practical action steps. But the best part is the lists of resources, information and agencies to help parents and teens navigate the many questions they need to consider.

This is a book that every minister, NOEL Chapter, Point Person and pro-lifer should have extra copies of to give when a friend or parishioner shares the news that their teenager is pregnant.

The author, Linda Perry, has been the Executive Director of the Assist Pregnancy Center in Annandale, Virginia, for more than ten years, and counseled hundreds of families through unexpected teen pregnancies. It is clear from her writing that she has seen the Lord turn a parent's sorrow to joy as they seek God's help. Her words offer hope.

How To Survive Your Teen's Pregnancy Practical Advice for a Christian Family is an important resource to save girls from choosing abortion. The book's message is loud and clear for both parent and teen once pregnancy has occurred, don't condemn and punish, instead offer forgiveness and support, and everyone will survive.
--Georgette Forney, Anglicans for Life

How To Survive Your Teen's Pregnancy

Practical Advice for the Parents of a Pregnant Christian Single

Linda Ellen Perry and
Lynellen D. S. Perry

Second Edition

Chalfont House
PO Box 84
Dumfries, Virginia
571-437-6163
www.ChalfontHouse.com

How To Survive Your Teen's Pregnancy: Practical Advice for the Parents of a Pregnant Christian Single. By Linda Ellen Perry and Lynellen D. S. Perry. Second Edition.

Published by:
Chalfont House, Post Office Box 84, Dumfries, VA 22026 USA
Info@ChalfontHouse.com   http://www.ChalfontHouse.com

Scripture quotations marked (MES) are taken from The Message. Copyright © by Eugene H. Peterson 1993, 1994, 1995. Used by permission of NavPress Publishing Group.

Scripture quotations marked (NASB) are taken from the NEW AMERICAN STANDARD BIBLE®, Copyright © 1960, 1962, 1963, 1968, 1971, 1972, 1973, 1975, 1977, 1995 by The Lockman Foundation. Used by permission.

Scripture quotations marked (NIV) are taken from the HOLY BIBLE, NEW INTERNATIONAL VERSION®. NIV®. Copyright © 1973, 1978, 1984 by the International Bible Society. Used by permission of Zondervan Publishing House. All rights reserved.

ISBN 978-0-9720111-5-0
First Printing 2007
Printed in the United States of America

Perry, Linda Ellen, 1942-   and Lynellen D. S. Perry, 1971 -
How To Survive Your Teen's Pregnancy: Practical Advice for the Parents of a Pregnant Christian Single.
1. Teenage mothers - United States - Life skills guides
2. Motherhood - Religious aspects - Christianity
3. Teenage pregnancy.   I. Title
HQ759.4.S26 2003
306.7088055

To Dennis,
Lynellen and Michael, and
Elizabeth and Timothy.
Thank you for the gift of family.

In memory of our parents,
Henry Alexander Jones (1874-1951)
and A. Mae Reavis (1906-1985),
C.H. Perry (1916 - 2004)
and Amanda Johnson (1921 - 2003).
Thank you for the gift of life.

Glory to God from whom
all blessings flow!

Acknowledgments

From Linda Perry

Thank you to Lynellen D.S. Perry and Elizabeth Maddrey for their typing, editing, and creative additions to the manuscript. What a blessing it is to be the mother and friend of two such beautiful young ladies. They are my most valued consultants. I am deeply grateful to Jesus for the priviledge of their companionship, support, and stimulation, and I'm pleased by their dedication to Christ. Thank you for bringing me such wonderful sons in Michael Perry and Timothy Maddrey.

I praise God for my precious husband, Dr. Dennis Gordon Perry. He is my best friend, most consistent supporter, and most valued ally.

With gratitude to the memory of my mother, Mae Reavis Jones Graham, for her training.

Thank you to special friends who provided inspiration and encouragement during the writing of this book.

I thank the Lord for Assist Pregnancy Center which has provided me with the opportunity to meet hundreds of families who have turned the sorrow of an unexpected pregnancy into joy with their willingness to give the gift of life. Many thanks to the board, staff, volunteers, and supporters of Assist who make ministry to "the least of these" rewarding.

May God receive all praise for any value found in this book.

Introduction to the Second Edition

When we wrote the manuscript for the first edition in 2002, there were very few reports and studies that had yet been published based on the 2000 Census data. We felt bad referencing so many sources that were published in the late 80s and the 1990s because they were very dated by the time the first edition went to the printer. We are very proud to have updated all the statistics throughout the second edition! In every case (but one) we were able to find a source reference from this millenium, and this make the second edition very fresh and timely.

We've also added new material throughout the book, especially a chapter about the importance of a father. We expanded the information about the grief cycle, and added some new illustrations. We love hearing from you, dear reader, and we thank you in advance for the comments and personal stories that you'll send us regarding this new edition.

Please browse our website for other resources that may be of benefit to you: www.ChalfontHouse.com

May God bless you and keep you.

Table of Contents

A Note To The Reader

You have found yourself in the middle of a crisis: the crisis of your single daughter's pregnancy. You never expected your family would be involved in a trauma of this magnitude. You are disappointed, angry, and searching for a way out. One often has little time and a limited attention span in the midst of a crisis. I hope God will use this book to bring hope and some practical suggestions for action.

Feel free to read chapters out of order - most of them are not overly dependent on the previous material. If you see a subject in the Table of Contents that seems to speak to your needs for the day, go ahead and read that chapter. You will probably want to make sure that you read every chapter (perhaps simply for your own educational purposes) at some point.

In the difficult days ahead as your daughter progresses in her pregnancy, she will be making decisions about giving birth vs. abortion, parenting vs. adoption, marriage vs. remaining single, continuing school vs. finding a job, and your involvement (as grandparents) in possibly raising your grandchild. There are no problems too big for God. I have found over and over again that if I will take time to listen, God will offer direction and a path out of my problems.

Since 1970, I have been concerned with the issues surrounding unplanned pregnancies. Since 1990, I have been the Executive Director of a Pregnancy Center in the suburbs of Northern Virginia. This opportunity has allowed me to be involved in the lives of pregnant single women, and often I have counseled with their parents.

I will be sharing from the testimonies of parents who have successfully turned the ashes of an unexpected pregnancy into joy and beauty. Pseudonyms are used to protect the identities of their families and some details have been changed.

As the mother of two adult daughters, I have experienced the joy and anxieties that come with raising girls in today's culture. It is my prayer that as we examine the issues surrounding an unplanned pregnancy the Lord will fulfill the promise in Isaiah 61:1-3,

"The Spirit of the Lord God is upon me,
Because the LORD has anointed me
To bring good news to the afflicted;
He has sent me to bind up the brokenhearted,
To proclaim liberty to captives,
And freedom to prisoners;
To proclaim the favorable year of the Lord,
And the day of vengeance of our God;
To comfort all who mourn,
To grant those who mourn in Zion,
Giving them a garland instead of ashes,
The oil of gladness instead of mourning,
A mantle of praise
        instead of a spirit of fainting.
So they will be called oaks of righteousness,
The planting of the Lord,
That He may be glorified." (NASB)

1. Hearing The Shocking News

I loathe my own life; I will give full vent to my complaint; I will speak in the bitterness of my soul. Job 10:1 (NASB)

Suggested Reading:　　Job 3　　　　Job's Lament

Job donned sackcloth and ashes to mourn the drastic change in his life circumstances. His friends, who should have been a consolation, came with confusion, doubts, and accusations. If you have just discovered that your single daughter is pregnant, you can probably identify with Job.

Pregnancy outside marriage is a common challenge in America today. In fact, the CDC notes that births to single mothers reached a record high in 2005. Many parents face the crisis of having their grandchildren born to a single mom, so you are not alone. However, it is probably little consolation to be told that 342,976 teens (aged 15-19) gave birth in 2005, or that more than one in three of all children born in America are born out of wedlock (36.8% in 2005) [1]. 69.5% of the children in the African American community are born to single mothers, as are 63.3% of children in the American Indian or Alaska Native population, and 47.9% of children with Hispanic mothers [1].

Job faced his problems alone with a few friends. I hope that this book will provide you with insights from many years of working with parents who have found themselves faced with the heartache and joy of the birth of their grandchild to an single mother. Just as thousands of other parents have survived this complicated and difficult situation, you too will survive. God's desire is to take the hurt and sorrow of these circumstances and provide opportunities for growth and even joy.

Jean says that when she learned that her 17-year-old high school senior was pregnant, "I felt like I had been hit square in the face with a 2x4. The shock and pain left me dazed. This was my model child, my spirit-filled child, whose Bible was worn. She was a member of the National Honor

Society, and determined to retain her virginity until marriage. The father of the baby was five years her senior and her first love. They had broken up and this [pregnancy] was [the result of] a chance meeting."

Joy's experience with her 21-year-old daughter, a junior in college, was similar. "When our daughter called us to tell us she was pregnant, I responded immediately with 'No, not you! I know what you've been taught.' My husband returned home during the conversation, and I had to relay to him this most difficult and unexpected news. Our feelings ranged from grief to rage, and back again. We talked and cried most of the night. At first he didn't want her to come home for the summer, but both of us realized that we needed one another. For a few days we wondered if we would live through it. We not only lived through it, but we also recovered from it."

Notes:
[1] National Vital Statistics Reports, Volume 55, Number 11, December 28, 2006. http://www.cdc.gov/nchs/data/nvsr/nvsr55/nvsr55_11.pdf

Prayer:
Heavenly Father, You know our circumstances. I recognize that you have plans for the future of everyone involved. Help me resist depression and bitterness as I lay my problems before you. I ask You for refuge and help in my time of trouble.

To Do:
Journaling is an important part of this devotional workbook because writing aids in clarifying your thoughts and emotions. It can even be a record of decisions as they are made. If you do not plan to write in this workbook then buy a journal or make a binder with paper where you will write about your experiences. Journal about these questions:

What is the thing that most concerns you right now?

What is your greatest hope?

Who has been a help so far?

What are your emotions right now?

The grief or trauma model includes emotions which will appear and reappear throughout your daughter's pregnancy.

Grief/Trauma model:

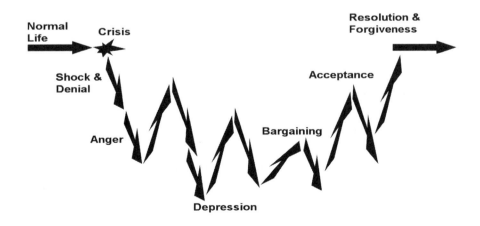

Where in the grief model are you now? How can you move on?

List the other people involved in this problem. What emotions do you see them experiencing?

Keep a log of daily prayer requests here and in your journal: (e.g. Help me to realize that each member of my family is upset. Help me to be able to see past my own hurt.)

Everyone involved in your daughter's life can experience the grief emotions to some degree. It might be good to go through the following exercise [3] as a family.

Recognizing Healing Is A Process

This exercise will help you examine the grief/trauma healing process. It will also help you to remember that emotions may resurface after you thought you had dealt with them. They can be triggered in various ways (e.g., seasons, music, people, babies, places, hormones, etc.). In the questions below, see if you can remember when you felt certain emotions and what triggered them in your heart.

Denial may be summarized by silence and inaction, ignoring the thoughts, feelings, and pain surrounding your daughter's pregnancy. Psalm 32:3 says, "When I kept silent about my sin, my body wasted away through my groaning all day long." What things (people, sights, sounds, smells, etc.) have triggered feelings of denial in you?

While we may be able to deny a pregnancy for a time, God knows about each of our actions, as seen in Psalm 90:8, "You have placed our iniquities before You, our secret sins in the light of Your presence." Denial only delays the healing process and the time when we can experience God's forgiveness. In Psalm 142:1-2, David is hiding in a cave: "I cry aloud with my voice to the Lord; I make supplication with my voice to the Lord. I pour out my complaint before Him; I declare my trouble before Him." In this verse, what does David do to combat denial?

Anger is either directed outward towards others, or inward towards yourself. Outward-directed anger can turn into bitterness or hatred over time. Inward-directed anger can become depression. Let's examine David's anger in Psalm 10:1, 3, 5, 6, 7, 8. David is complaining that life doesn't seem fair. What is David specifically angry about in each verse?

Psalm 10:1

Psalm 10:3

Psalm 10:5

Psalm 10:7

Psalm 10:8

Have you had any of these symptoms of prolonged anger? (Check all that apply):

____ Abdominal pain	____ Intestinal disorder
____ Headaches	____ Anxiety attacks
____ Heart disorder	____ Muscle tension
____ Relationship problems	____ Irritability
____ Breathing disorder	____ High blood pressure
____ Sleep disorder	____ Impatience
____ Uncontrolled outbursts	____ Compulsive behaviors

Did you know that God gets angry, too? Psalm 78:49-50 was written about the Israelites continuously rebelling in the desert and says, "He (God) sent upon them His burning anger, fury, and indignation, and trouble, a band of destroying angels. He leveled a path for His anger; He did not spare their soul from death, but gave over their life to the plague." God created the emotion of anger, so anger itself is not a sin but the actions we take while angry are often sinful. Ephesians 4:26 says, "Be angry, but do not sin. Do not let the sun go down on your anger." What people or things trigger your feelings of anger about this pregnancy?

Depression is often defined as "anger turned inward over time." David and other Biblical authors expressed depression at times. Underline the depression feelings and behaviors as described in Psalm 22:1, 2, 6, and 15:

(1) My God, my God, why have You forsaken me? Far from my deliverance are the words of my groaning. (2) O my God, I cry by day, but You do not answer; and by night, but I have no rest. (6) But I am a worm and not a man, a reproach of men and despised by the people. (15) My strength is dried up like a potsherd, and my tongue cleaves to my jaws; and You lay me in the dust of death.

What people or things trigger your feelings of depression about this pregnancy?

The next stage of the grief model is bargaining. A bargain is a vow or statement like "If <Party A> does <Action A> then <Party B> will do

<Action B>." Here's an example. Genesis 28:20-21, "Then Jacob made a vow, saying, 'If God will be with me and will keep me on this journey that I take, and will give me food to eat and garments to wear, and I return to my father's house in safety, then the Lord will be my God.'"

What bargains have you attempted to make with God about this pregnancy?

What bargains have you tried to make with people about this pregnancy?

Once you recognize your pain trigger points, spend time in prayer asking the Lord to protect you from overwhelming emotions. Understand these feelings are normal. Think of ways you can face these emotions constructively. In times of stress, alert the people closest to you that this is a sensitive time. Ask them to be considerate, supportive, and to pray for you. The only way out of the crisis pit of anger, depression, and bargaining is to move toward healing by first accepting the situation. Accept your past decisions, any responsibility you bear as well as the role of others, and accept that you cannot change the past. Part of acceptance is to confess any sin you've contributed to the situation. 1 John 1:9 says "If we confess our sins, He is faithful and just to forgive us our sins and cleanse us from all unrighteousness." Accept God's forgiveness after you've confessed to Him, and don't hold a grudge against yourself or others.

Finally, at the resolution stage of the grief cycle one would hope to arrive at a higher level of coping than one had before the crisis began. If healing has occurred, one should at least arrive back at the same level of function. The healing process may take some time. Do not demand instantaneous healing in your life. We pray that this book will help you through the stages of the grief cycle and that you and your family will learn new skills that help you heal and even strengthen your relationships.

2. The Importance Of First Words

No test or temptation that comes your way is beyond the course of what others have had to face. All you need to remember is that God will never let you down; he'll never let you be pushed past your limit; he'll always be there to help you come through it. 1 Corinthians 10:13 (MES)

Suggested Reading: Matthew 18:15-20   Handling Problems

One of the first thoughts that comes into our minds is "What did I do to deserve this heartbreak?" You may also feel discouragement, guilt, shame, anger, and a need to blame someone. All of these reactions are normal, but none of these reactions is helpful. The first words you say to your daughter will be remembered for a long time. Start the practice of thinking carefully and praying before you speak.

Jean writes, "My first reaction was to say 'How dare you! This was not the way that I wanted to become a grandparent!' But God immediately provided a cooling-off period for me so that I didn't react to that first impulse: the doorbell rang within 30 seconds of my daughter telling me she was pregnant. So I had to put on my 'I'm-all-together' mask. When the visitor finally left I was able to take my daughter in my arms and tell her I loved her and that we would get through this together."

You need to assure your daughter you love her. Yes, you are disappointed and hurt, but she is still valued. Cry together, pray, and start making plans to help her and her child.

Families in your church, your neighborhood, and your community are experiencing similar pains. Many pregnancy resource centers (PRCs) offer support groups and counseling for the parents of pregnant teenagers. One of the key ingredients in growing through this crisis experience is joining together with others for support. It might be good to make a list of individuals in your community who have faced a similar problem. If there's no support group already organized, you could ask your pastor to call no more than eight of these individuals and see if they are willing to meet together to share concerns and resources.

Even if you have always been against abortion, expect Satan to tempt you with the lie that abortion will erase the pregnancy. Parents have confessed to me in abortion recovery classes that they forced their children to abort, thinking the abortion would spare the family pain. Instead they have found they had a dead grandchild and a broken-hearted son or daughter.

There are many reasons that teens get pregnant. Here are a few possibilities that you can discuss with your daughter. To what extent does she feel any of these was a factor in her becoming pregnant?

• Young women may be a victim of someone who exploited her innocence (see Appendix A for possible action to take). A 2004 study found that 44% of high school students think that boys at their school often or sometimes "push girls to drink alcohol or take drugs in order to get the girls to have sex or do other sexual things" [2].

• Young women could feel that pregnancy will guarantee marriage.

• She may want to hold onto a guy.

• She may feel unloved by her parents.

• She may be angry at her parents and want to punish or hurt them.

• She may have had inadequate training in spiritual and moral issues.

• She may have a lack of commitment to God and to the moral and spiritual issues she has been taught.

• She may want to be accepted by the crowd.

• She may have a lack of goals and is drifting.

• She may intentionally get pregnant with an "atonement child" to replace a child aborted previously.

Luther McIntyre says, "After our daughter told us she was pregnant, the thing I thought most about was not her mistake, but my own long history of mistakes and failures" [1]. Both parents in today's chapter recognized they too had sinned and they stood with their daughters as they faced the future. At this stage, Luther McIntyre found it helpful to take a piece of paper and list all of the sins of his daughter. In the next column he made a list of his own sins. This helped him to remember that he too was an individual in need of God's mercy and helped him recognize how much the Lord had forgiven him.

Notes:

[1] Help for Hurting Parents: Dealing with the Pain of Teen Pregnancy. Luther McIntyre. Good Life Publishing, 1997. Page 3. This personal and true story is out of print. Other, similar, books that you might find encouraging include "I'm Pregnant, Now What?" (2004) by Ruth Graham and Sara Dormon; and "Mom, Dad... I'm Pregnant" (2004) by Jayne Schooler.
[2] "National Survey of American Attitudes on Substance Abuse IX: Teen Dating Practices and Sexual Activity". The National Center on Addiction and Subtance Abuse (CASA) at Columbia University. www. casacolumbia.org

Note that "PRC" is used throughout the book to stand for "Pregnancy Resource Center". Other typical names for this type of ministry to pregnant women and their families are "Crisis Pregnancy Center" (CPC), "Pregnancy Help Center" (PHC) and "Pregnancy Care Center" (PCC).

Prayer:

I thank you, Lord, for the testimonies of many parents who have wept when given the news of their daughter's unexpected pregnancy but later rejoiced at your solution to their pain. Heavenly Father, calm my heart and help me to take one day at a time as my daughter and I seek to find your will step by step.

To Do:

Call 1-800-395-HELP to find your closest CareNet or Heartbeat PRC. Write the phone number of that PRC here:

Call your pastor or other mature Christian friend and ask for prayer. Write the name of the person you will call, and afterwards record any comments or phrases from the conversation that were encouraging to you.

Write out some items for each of these lists:

My sins this month   My daughter's sins this month

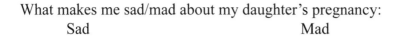

The Importance Of First Words

What makes me sad/mad about my daughter's pregnancy:
    Sad   Mad

The following list will take days, weeks, and months to grow. During the weeks ahead, re-read this list from time to time and see if there are additional items you can record. What makes me thankful in this situation (e.g., she told us of the pregnancy instead of getting a secret abortion):

Do you remember any hurtful conversations with your parents when you were young? What did they say that hurt you?

Do you remember any encouraging conversations with your parents when you were young? What did they say that helped you?

What were the first things you said to your daughter?

Do you need to apologize to her and ask for forgiveness?

If you could go back in time and have that first conversation again, what would you like to say (instead of what you actually said)?

What words would be an encouragement to your daughter now?

Tape a picture of your family or daughter on this page. Every time you see this picture, think of times of happiness and blessing while you pray for each family member.

3. Supporting My Daughter as She Makes Decisions

Come to me, all you who are weary and burdened, and I will give you rest. Take my yoke upon you and learn from me, for I am gentle and humble in heart, and you will find rest for your souls. For my yoke is easy and my burden is light. Matthew 11:29-30 (NIV)

Suggested Reading: Matthew 11:25-30   Jesus Lifts Burdens

It is important for your daughter to make an informed choice about her pregnancy. When a young woman is pregnant outside of marriage, there usually are no painless solutions. Any decision made brings its own problems and heartache. Obviously, I hope your daughter would never choose an abortion. But unless you live in a state which has a "parental consent" law, you are powerless to prevent her from making this traumatic choice. I have observed numerous girls who were forced into a abortion against their wishes. These girls often find themselves in another pregnancy very quickly. In abortion recovery ministry, the statistics show that the girl is often pregnant again within a year of the abortion. The guilt carried from the abortion seems to prompt these girls to seek an "atonement child." She dreams that, with this new child, she will be able to atone for the death of the previous child. If your daughter aborts your grandchild, please help her get abortion recovery counseling and healing afterwards and also seek grief counseling for yourself and other family members.

If your daughter chooses to parent the child herself, I trust she will communicate with you and seriously prepare herself for the realities of this choice. A PRC can help her understand what parenting involves on a daily basis. Many use an "Earn While You Learn" curriculum to prepare clients for parenting.

If your daughter chooses to make an adoption plan, it is important she write an adoption plan that includes all the steps, even those that will be taken at the hospital. I think it is always helpful to have a dedication/blessing service led by a spiritual advisor (your pastor, an elder, a youth leader, or simply a well-respected Christian friend) in which your daughter relinquishes the child (face to face) to the adoptive parents. This simple service can bring great closure to the new birthmother and her family.

The "atonement child" phenomenon is also found with girls who are forced to place their child in adoption. If she relinquishes a child against her will, she may quickly become pregnant again. This time she will be determined to stand up for her child and parent it. It is important that a PRC, adoption agency, or Christian professional provide counsel to a pregnant woman as early as possible in her pregnancy. This will allow her many months to examine her options and make a plan that she can live with for the rest of her life. You may enjoy reading the book "Atonement Child" by Francine Rivers. This is a fictional story of a family with three generations of pregnancy outside of marriage, but it is based on the experiences of Francine and her mother. Another book you may enjoy is "I'm Pregnant, Now What?" which records Ruth Graham's story about how her daughter got pregnant twice before marriage. She made an adoption plan for the first child, under pressure, and parented the second child. Ruth (daughter of Billy Graham) and her daughter felt they had few resources they could turn to for help.

If your daughter is planning to marry the father of her child, it is important to have the support and involvement of both families. Your parenting of your daughter is not an 18-year task but rather a privilege that lasts a lifetime. It is common for anyone facing a difficulty to operate in denial, putting off decisions until they absolutely have to be made. Decisions made at the last moment do not receive the careful thought and planning required for a good decision. As a parent, it is your responsibility to encourage your daughter to think through her options thoroughly and make an informed choice.

Prayer:
Lord our Righteousness (Jehovah Tsidkenu), we seek your face for wisdom and guidance as our daughter looks at her options for this pregnancy. Give us the grace to be supportive regardless of her decision. Give her the wisdom to make the decision that is your will for her life and for the life of her child.

To Do:
Write about the following topics.

Friends and family are urging us to …

I want my daughter to.....

I want my husband/family to...

Burdens I am carrying …

How I have found rest for my soul ...

To find a professional Christian counselor for your daughter, ask your church or a Christian friend for a referral. A local PRC may also have a referral list of Christian counselors. Finally, there is a searchable referral network at the website of the American Association of Christian Counselors (www.aacc.net). Write here the names and phone numbers of a few possible counselors:

Have your daughter research the consequences of adoption, parenting, and abortion. One website to explore is www.afterabortion.org, which has many articles, testimonies and research results about the effects of abortion (physically, emotionally, and spiritually). Your daughter should list the pros and cons of each option, and make lists of how the consequences are similar to each other and how they are different.

Make your own lists here.
Consquences of adoption:

Consequences of parenting:

Consequences of abortion:

Pros and cons of adoption:

Pros and cons of parenting:

Pros and cons of abortion:

How adoption and abortion are similar:

How adoption and abortion are different:

How adoption and parenting are similar:

How adoption and parenting are different:

How parenting and abortion are different:

4. First Steps To Take

Trust in the Lord with all your heart and lean not on your own under-standing; in all your ways acknowledge him, and he will make your paths straight. Proverbs 3:5-6 (NIV)

Suggested Reading: 2 Samuel 7:18-26   David's Prayer

When faced with an unexpectedly pregnant young woman, three of the first steps to take are:
1) Go to a local Pregnancy Resource Center (PRC) (call 1-800-395-HELP for a referral).
2) Take your daughter to an OBGYN to begin her prenatal health care and get tested for sexually transmitted diseases.
3) Decide whether to meet with the father of the baby, and his parents.

Pregnancy Help Centers
At a PRC you will find volunteers trained in dealing with unexpected pregnancies. The PRC is a free and confidential environment for your daughter's pregnancy test and ongoing counseling. The PRC is equipped to educate your daughter throughout her pregnancy on topics related to pregnancy, parenting, and adoption. They can often help with provid-ing maternity clothes, baby clothes, and furniture. They may even have ongoing single parent support groups. Developing a relationship with a local center can provide you with dependable long-term services. PRCs also give referrals to maternity homes, legal assistance, medical care, and other helpful agencies.

OBGYN Appointment
The PRC can give you a list of pro-life OBGYNs. Your daughter's first appointment can be stressful. It is important that she is referred to a pro-life doctor who will be supportive of her pregnancy. Some other doctors try to counsel single pregnant girls toward abortion. In states where there is no required waiting period or parental notification/consent law, they may even try to persuade her to have an abortion in the office at that very moment. Never take a young woman to get a pregnancy test at an abortion clinic or Planned Parenthood because of their abortion agenda.

Father of the Baby and His Parents

After you have evaluated your daughter's relationship with the father of the child and determined that it is appropriate for it to continue, you may wish to meet with him and his parents. Your daughter's feelings about the baby's father are primary here. If she does not want to meet with him or his parents, her wishes should be respected.

Choose a quiet and calm environment to talk to the expectant father and his parents. It may be helpful to have your pastor or a mature Christian friend at this meeting. Know what is going to be discussed and agree on it beforehand. Keep the first meeting's agenda simple. It should focus on getting to know each other and pledging support for the young couple.

After the first meeting, schedule a few more meetings. At these other meetings, it is important to listen thoughtfully to the feelings of the young people, giving advice only when asked. Listen to what the young people think should be the steps taken in regards to the preborn child. If the young man does not plan to act in a responsible manner, the girl's relationship with him should be ended.

These first steps are very important and should be taken gently, with much prayer and love. Other thoughts about this meeting are in the chapter titled "Forgiving The Baby's Father".

Prayer:

Loving Lord, help us to provide a supportive and loving environment for our daughter as she begins to take her first steps in planning for this unexpected pregnancy. Help the father and paternal grandparents to desire to be a help.

To Do:

What does our daughter desire concerning a meeting with the young man and his parents?

40

Decide on a safe, pleasant place for the meeting with the baby's father and his parents. Write here the location you chose:

Who should you invite to be a prayerful and helpful observer? (Pastor, friend, counselor, or someone who has been through this type of experience)

Decide on the "agenda" of the meeting. Purposes could be:
· To get to know each other.
· To have the young people tell what they plan to do (i.e., marriage, end their relationship, etc.).
· To discuss how the father wants to be involved.

Write out your meeting agenda here:

Invite the baby's father and his parents by phone, in person, by email, or in a note. In the invitation, outline the purpose of the meeting.

Complete these sentences:
What I hope will be accomplished during a meeting with the baby's father and his parents ...

What we accomplished at the meeting ...

As a result of the meeting, we should ...

Write about today's reading in 2 Samuel 7:18-26. How did these verses speak to you?

5. The Pregnancy Resource Center

Praise be to the God and Father of our Lord Jesus Christ, the Father of compassion and the God of all comfort, who comforts us in all our troubles, so that we can comfort those in any trouble with the comfort we ourselves have received from God. 2 Corinthians 1:3-4 (NIV)

Suggested reading: Psalm 27   Wait on the Lord

Over the years, many mothers of pregnant teens have expressed to me their appreciation for Assist Pregnancy Center, where I serve as Executive Director. Their comments have included statements such as:

"It was so good to have another responsible adult interacting with my daughter. It took a huge burden off my shoulders."

"I was glad I could trust the counselors to give my daughter sound Christian advice."

"This was the first time my daughter and I had ever been in a crisis of this magnitude. The counselors at the pregnancy center had seen similar situations many times. I felt confident in their ability to help."

"I was so appreciative of the kind, supportive, and non-judgmental attitude my daughter and I received at the pregnancy center. She made many friends."

Many PRCs have staff or volunteers who have either experienced a pregnancy outside of marriage in their family or with a close friend. Several of my volunteers over the years have been mothers who, grateful for the help they received with their pregnant daughters, came back to be counselors.

In Appendix D - Resources, you will see several sources to help you find a PRC located near you. Pregnancy Centers associated with CareNet,

Heartbeat International, and other life-affirming ministries have joined in standardizing the excellence at their Centers with a document called "Our Commitment to Care." A copy of this promise is included here.

Our Commitment to Care

1. We are dedicated to providing a warm and safe environment to everyone, regardless of your age, race, income, nationality, religious affiliation or circumstances.

2. You will be treated with kindness and compassion and may leave the pregnancy help center whenever you wish.

3. Your story will be listened to with respect and courtesy and without judgment, ridicule or rejection.

4. You have the right to withhold any information you do not want to share with a volunteer. All information shared will be held in strict and absolute confidence, except in the rare circumstances when prohibited by law.

5. You will receive accurate information about pregnancy, fetal development, life-style issues and related concerns. Assist CPC does not provide abortion or referrals for abortion, but we are committed to offering accurate information about abortion procedures and risks.

6. You may refuse any information you do not wish to receive.

7. You will receive honest and open answers.

8. You will be directed to other appropriate resources that could support you in your time of crisis and supply you with additional help and information.

9. You will be given ongoing support in accordance with your needs.

The services offered at most pregnancy centers include: pregnancy tests;

factual and complete information about abortion and its risks, fetal development, prenatal health care, parenting skills, labor and childbirth, sexually transmitted diseases, adoption, spiritual growth, abortion recovery, and education on sexual integrity. Many Centers also offer referrals for medical and legal help, maternity clothing, baby clothing and supplies, baby furniture, and parenting support groups. Some Centers offer job skills training. Some Centers offer limited medical services such as ultrasounds and testing for sexually transmitted diseases. All Centers offer their services confidentially and free of charge. I'm sure you will find a Center near you to provide outstanding support and help.

Prayer:
Lord Who Sticks Closer Than a Brother, thank You for preparing helpers to walk alongside us during this challenging journey. We thank You that, because of this experience, we have the opportunity to grow in You.

To Do:
Start (or add to) a memory book of your daughter's pregnancy.

Read books to the younger children in your family about prenatal life or pregnancy. For example: The Amazing Beginning of You by Matt and Lisa Jacobson.

Write about the following topics:
What impressed you as you read "Our Commitment to Care"?

What PRC services do you need?

What services does your daughter need?

Add prayer requests and answers:

6. The Doctor Appointment

The Lord is my strength and my shield; my heart trusts in him, and I am helped. My heart leaps for joy and I will give thanks to him in song. Psalm 28:7 (NIV)

Suggested reading: Psalm 28   God Hears My Prayer

If your daughter is a minor or a full-time student, her medical expenses may be covered under your insurance. Contact your insurance representative to get information about the procedures for covering your daughter's pregnancy. If you have a policy that allows you to pick your own doctor, ask the PRC for a list of pro-life doctors in your area. You can also get a referral from either The American Association of Pro-Life Obstetricians and Gynecologists (www.aaplog.org) or The Christian Medical and Dental Associations (www.cmda.org) (ask if the doctor is pro-life in addition to being a Christian).

If your daughter is not covered under your medical insurance, sometimes a doctor will have a sliding fee scale or you may be eligible for help from your local government's social services. Some pregnancy centers and churches have accounts to help with uncovered medical expenses, and some PRCs offer medical services directly.

It is important for your daughter's first OBGYN appointment to take place with a doctor who will affirm her pregnancy and the value of the child she is carrying. The counseling at a Planned Parenthood or other abortion-minded facilities can raise needless questions in the mind of your daughter. One of the sad results of the Roe v. Wade decision in 1973 is that pregnant women are routinely asked if they plan to terminate the pregnancy or carry to term. This can be a devastating question for a vulnerable young woman.

The first visit to the doctor will confirm several important facts. You will learn the gestational age of the child and the expected date of birth. Your daughter will be encouraged to practice a healthy lifestyle which will include proper nutrition, exercise and sleep. She needs to refrain from tobacco, alcohol, drugs, and avoid even most over-the-counter medicines. She may also be given pre-natal vitamins and a schedule of future doctor's visits. Your daughter should absolutely be tested for sexually transmitted diseases (STDs) as soon as possible.

It is advisable for you to attend the appointment with your daughter even if you are not allowed into the examining room. Your daughter can request for you to be present during the exam. Your presence will provide the encouragement and support your daughter needs. You will have the opportunity to ask questions and receive education about ways to help your daughter during the pregnancy.

Many women of all ages don't know about the normal progression of a healthy pregnancy. Pregnancy education will help your daughter cope with the changes in her body. There are hundreds of pregnancy books available, so read reviews of a variety of books before selecting a couple to purchase. As mentioned before, most PRCs can offer you very a good pregnancy education curriculum.

Prayer:
Dear All-Sufficient One (El Shaddai), I lift up to You the health of my daughter and my grandchild. Grant us compassionate care from encouraging medical workers. We trust You to provide for all of us emotionally, physically, and spiritually.

To Do:
Check your health insurance coverage to see how it applies to your daughter's pregnancy. If your daughter isn't covered on your insurance, a PRC can refer you to other options: Some doctors and hospitals have sliding fees; some states offer health insurance for teens and their babies, etc. A PRC can also give you information about Public Assistance coverage. Write here some notes about your daughter's medical insurance situation for this pregnancy:

Do some research on the Internet to discover the effects of drugs, alcohol and tobacco on the preborn child and the child's development throughout its life. Write notes on your findings here:

Check with your daughter for any accountability she wants you to give her. For example, in the areas of giving up drugs, alcohol, tobacco, caffeine, etc. Also, in the areas of adding healthy exercise, diet, and sleep to her life. Write here the items for which she wants accountability:

Journal about today's reading from Psalm 28 by writing out the statements that talk about who God is:

Write out David's pleas to God:

Write about what you learned from this Psalm:

7. Where Will We Be in a Year?

The fear of the LORD is the beginning of wisdom, and the knowledge of the Holy One is understanding. Proverbs 9:10 (NIV)

Suggested Reading: Proverbs 9   Wisdom or Folly?

As your daughter works through her pregnancy, she should be spending time considering the future. Certainly the decisions she makes (about marrying, parenting the child, or making an adoption plan) will have a huge impact on her future plans but if she has an abortion the consequences spiritually, emotionally, and physically are likely to be traumatic.

A child is born after nine full months in the womb. This can be a productive time for an evaluation of the next year or year and a half. Depending on the age of your daughter, some of the decisions that need to be made are as follows. Sit down with your daughter to discuss the following questions about the next year of life. Make notes on your answers to these questions:

· Where will she finish high school or college?

· Are these months of pregnancy instead a time for job training?

· Will she be working part time or full time while pregnant? How about after the baby is born?

· What was her career goal prior to pregnancy?

· Was it a realistic career goal? If not, what careers would she like to pursue now?

· What arrangements for childcare are available while she works or attends school?

· Where (and with whom) will she live during the pregnancy? After the baby is born?

· What is the maturity level of her spiritual life?

· Does your daughter spend time regularly studying the Bible and in prayer?

· Is she in fellowship with a Christian group that provides accountability?

· Has she truly repented of her premarital sexual activity and dedicated herself to a life of purity until she marries?

· How can you help her avoid sexual temptation in the future?

· Do friends who are making wrong choices influence your daughter?

· What conclusions can be drawn by examining her lifestyle in terms of books, music, TV, and film?

A formula I like to use when evaluating decisions is:

1. Were my actions and thoughts in accordance with what the Bible teaches? (The Ten Commandments are a good starting point. Exodus 20:7-17).

2. Do I know the voice of the Holy Spirit as He speaks to my conscience? Do I obey His promptings?

3. Do I go along with the crowd and the culture, or do I lean against it and follow God's way when there is a conflict?

4. Do I know what my personality and decision making characteristics are? Do I seek to know if God wants me to move outside of my comfort zone?

In examining the next 18 months, faith and fellowship will be extremely important. Your daughter should understand the practical realities of God's commands. The Ten Commandments and the Golden Rule are a good place to start. She should fellowship with people her own age (and older) whom she can trust. They can act as mature sounding boards willing to offer Godly advice to help her in days to come.

Prayer:
Lord, help us to seek Your face in order to find wisdom and understanding. Help us to avoid the folly of following our culture.

To Do:

Look in a dictionary for the meaning of wisdom and of folly. Based on the dictionary,

Wisdom is …   Folly is …

Read Proverbs 9 and fill out these two lists:

Wisdom is …   Folly is …

Write down the decisions that must be made in the next 18 months. Arrange them in order, and give them a possible target date.

Decisions that must be made: Target date:

With your daughter, create a Life Line diagram covering the previous 18 months of her life. List good decisions above the line, and bad decisions below it. It might be beneficial for your daughter to discuss this timeline with a Christian counselor who can help her evaluate her thought processes and decision-making skills.

Good
_____
Bad

How and why has your daughter made the bad decisions?

What helped her make good decisions?

Do you think she might make different decisions if she evaluated her thoughts using a formula like the one presented in this chapter?

The 13-week "Truth Project" by Focus on the Family (www.TruthProject. org) will help your family examine their worldview to see if it is Biblical. See if your family can attend the Truth Project series together.

Seek career counseling for your daughter. This may be available at her school. Larry Burkett (www.crown.org) also has tests available to help an individual look at their personality type and good career fits.

8. Restoring Sexual Integrity

Therefore, if anyone is in Christ, he is a new creation; the old has gone, the new has come! 2 Corinthians 5:17 (NIV)

Suggested Reading: John 8:1 – 11   The Adulterous Woman

When there has been a sexual relationship, two lives have been made one as the Scripture promised 'the two have been made one flesh' (Ephesians 5:31). In order to start over again it is necessary to make a break with the past.

Breaking the connection between former sexual partners can be a long and difficult process. Parents can support this process. If you don't have a relationship with your daughter that includes sexual accountability, seek the help of a youth leader or mature Christian friend. Your daughter's first step to a new lifestyle is the determination she wants to be free of the bondage of the past sexual relationship. Then she must deliberately act upon this decision. We can use the acronym "ACTS" to outline the process to freedom.

First, your daughter must **Acknowledge** her sin to herself and to others. Psalm 32:5 states, "Then I let it all out; I said, 'I'll make a clean breast of my failures to God.' Suddenly the pressure was gone – my guilt dissolved, my sin disappeared." (MES)

Sin must be **Confessed** to God and to those who have been affected by the sin. 1 John 1:9 reminds us, "If we admit our sins – make a clean breast of them – he won't let us down; he'll be true to himself. He'll forgive our sins and purge us of all wrongdoing" (MES). Some of the people who should receive an acknowledgement of her sin include: her family, her siblings, her boyfriend and his parents, and possibly the church and/ or youth group. This is a difficult step to take but it can have powerful results. Your daughter can see the forgiveness and love of those she has wronged. She can receive restoration and accountability from her spiritual family.

Next, **Thank** God for the forgiveness He gives and for the power He gives us to resist sin in the future. "No test or temptation that comes your way is beyond the course of what others have had to face. All you need to remember is that God will never let you down; he'll never let you be pushed past your limit; he'll always be there to help you come through it." 1 Corinthians 10:13 (MES).

James 1:12-15 tells us, "Don't let anyone under pressure to give in to evil say 'God is trying to trip me up.' God is impervious to evil, and puts evil in no one's way. The temptation to give in to evil comes from us and only us. We have no one to blame but the leering, seducing flare up of our own lust. Lust gets pregnant, and has a baby: sin! Sin grows up to adulthood, and becomes a real killer" (MES). This powerful promise can encourage your daughter that even if there has been a long sexual relationship God is powerful enough to help her recover sexual integrity. A person with restored sexual integrity is one who has been engaged in sexual sin but now comes before the Lord declaring the desire to remain sexually pure until marriage.

Finally, your daughter must **Seek** a lifestyle that pleases God in her thoughts and actions. We are reminded in Hebrews 4:15-16, "Now that we know we have – Jesus, this great High Priest with ready access to God – let's not let it slip through our fingers. We don't have a priest who is out of touch with our reality. He's been through weakness and testing, experienced it all – all but the sin. So let's walk right up to him and get what he's so ready to give. Take the mercy, accept the help" (MES).

Your daughter needs to have an accountability group that will encourage her in her desire to save her next sexual relationship for marriage. If your church has an abstinence or chastity vow service, participate with your daughter. If they do not, have a commitment service within your family and present her with a gift that is a symbol of her vow to the Lord.

Prayer:
Lord, my Banner (Jehovah Nissi), we thank You that You are God and that You forgive. You promise to bury our sins in the depths of the ocean and put them as far from us as the east is from the west. We are grateful You

don't remember anymore. We thank You that you can give us the power to resist temptation and sin. We pray that You will give our daughter the strength she needs to be sexually pure until she is married. We rest on You the banner of our victory over the enemy, Satan.

To Do:

Ask your daughter if she is ready to repent and change her lifestyle. If she is not ready to acknowledge her sin and change, the days ahead will be more difficult for all involved.

Some activities that can be used with your daughter as she relinquishes sexual ties include:

· Find some rocks, one for each boy with whom she has had sex. Write the name of one boy onto each rock. She should carry the rocks in her pocket for a day to remind her of the burden that came with the sexual involvement. At the end of the day, the stones can be prayed over and then thrown into a lake, stream, or ocean. Ask the Lord to break the soul connection between her and the sexual partner as she throws the stone into the water.

· Write out the various sinful relationships and activities on paper. Make a simple cross out of sticks or a floral form and nail (or tack) the confession to the cross with prayer. The confession can then be burned or shredded.

· Help your daughter to understand the stages of physical intimacy:
      Eye to Body, Eye to Eye, Voice to Voice
      Hand to Hand, Arm around Shoulder, Arm around Waist
      Touching face and simple kissing
      French Kissing
      Touching breasts or genitals
      Intercourse

Help your daughter decide what stage of intimacy will be her new boundary until she is married. Encourage her to choose a boundary line that is as far away from intercourse as possible. Once a couple has reached the stage of foreplay, it is quite difficult for them to stop the head-long rush of physical intimacy.

· When your daughter resumes dating activities, encourage her to help you set curfews and limitations on activities. You may decide together that she will not view films with explicit sexual scenes or read romance novels containing graphic descriptions of sexual encounters.

· Some single moms have found it helpful to state at the beginning of a new relationship that they have made a vow before God to be pure until marriage. The young man needs to agree to this before she will date him.

Decide how to acknowledge your daughters sexual integrity vow. Research has shown that a public vow to remain pure will postpone sexual involvement. Choose a gift that will serve as a symbol of her vow. There are many rings and necklaces designed for this purpose. Write here about your plans to acknowledge her sexual integrity vow:

Choose a resource or two that will educate your daughter on sexual purity and give her the courage to be pure until marriage. The Abstinence Clearinghouse has many great resources from which to select (www. abstinence.net).

9. Completing School

Do your best to present yourself to God as one approved, a workman who does not need to be ashamed and who correctly handles the word of truth. 2 Timothy 2:15 (NIV)

Suggested Reading: 2 Timothy 2:14-26   An Approved Worker

Early in the pregnancy you must decide where your daughter will complete her school year. Most school districts will allow a student to continue in their own school throughout the pregnancy. If your daughter would prefer not to continue with her current classmates, she may have several alternative options: going to night school, transferring to a special school, or completing her work via tutoring or home schooling. Her school guidance counselor will be able to discuss the options that are available in your area.

Some public school districts allow a pregnant young woman to take the bare essentials and waive the elective courses not needed for a diploma. This allows the student to graduate early. Night school often has the core classes needed for graduation, though they may not have all the electives available during the day. If your daughter is planning to go to college, it is important for her to continue to take the classes she will need to meet entrance requirements.

Many public school districts have special schools for young people with problems such as pregnancy. There are advantages to attending such a school:

· Generally the curriculum is pared down to the essentials in order to allow an accelerated completion timeframe.

· The school nurse may provide weekly prenatal checkups.

· The curriculum may include parenting classes.

· A practicum time in the school nursery of caring for infants born to classmates may be part of the curriculum.

· After the baby is born, your daughter may be able to take her child to school with her. The hour of childcare would then be devoted to caring for her own child instead of someone else's.

Homeschooling is another viable option, with many choices in curriculum. You or other family members may serve as teacher for various classes, or the school district may provide a tutor for a few hours a day to evaluate the independent work performed by your daughter. Another option is online learning. Your daughter's lessons can be graded by the computer or a teacher located elsewhere.

With all of these options available, there is no excuse for your daughter to fail to complete at least high school. If your daughter has poor academic skills or no interest in receiving a diploma, she can study for the GED equivalency test. Community colleges will generally allow students with a GED to enroll.

Obviously, if your daughter is already in college when she becomes pregnant, you will need to discover if there are any policies that prohibit her from continuing her education. Some Christian colleges do not allow single pregnant students to remain in school. Many colleges are now adding online courses to their curriculum. Perhaps your daughter could enroll for one or two semesters online so that she isn't on campus during her pregnancy.

About one-third of female high school dropouts in America today cite pregnancy as the reason they stopped going to school [1]. It is important that you affirm the life-long values of education which will benefit not only your daughter but her child. Gather around you a group of supportive people who will encourage and aid your daughter in finishing (at minimum) her high school education.

Notes:

[1] "The Silent Epidemic: Perspectives of High School Dropouts" by

John Bridgeland, John Dilulio, Jr., and Karen Burke Morison. March 2006. Report by Civic Enterprises. www.civicenterprises.net

Prayer:

All-Wise God, we ask for Your grace to enable our daughter to be a diligent student. Help her complete her education so that her future has more hope and promise.

To Do:

With your daughter, speak to a counselor at her school about her educational options. Record here any notes from that conversation.

Discuss the educational options with your daughter and listen carefully to her ideas. What are her main thoughts?

What were her educational plans before the pregnancy?

What would it take to help your daughter realize her educational and career dreams?

Consider career testing if your daughter has no idea of her educational goals. Tests are available online from Crown Financial Ministries (www. crown.org) or other Christian financial experts.

10. Trying To Hide

Friends love through all kinds of weather, and families stick together in all kinds of trouble. Proverbs 17:17 (MES)

Suggested Reading: 2 Samuel 11   David and Bathsheba

Parents often wonder what people will say when they hear about their daughter's pregnancy. In a previous chapter, "The Importance of First Words," you made a list of your daughter's recent sins and your own sins. Review your list of sins and put a "P" beside the ones that are public knowledge. Put an "S" by the secret sins only you know about.

If each of us were honest we would recognize that many times a day we have improper thoughts that the Lord considers sin. It is often tempting to not take our "secret" sins seriously or to not work hard to eradicate them. Secret sins may have lead to your daughter's pregnancy but as her pregnancy advances it will become more public. More and more people will become aware of the fact that she is carrying a baby.

Like David, you may be tempted to hide this sin. You may be considering an abortion. In years past (for we all know that out-of-wedlock pregnancy is an age-old problem) a girl faced few choices: either a quickie marriage; leaving home to have the baby elsewhere and placing the baby for adoption; or an illegal abortion. In 1973, the terrible option of abortion became legal. The Alan Guttmacher Institute (research department of major abortion provider Planned Parenthood) says that about half of all pregnancies in America were unexpected and that 42% of unexpected pregnancies end in abortion. Their survey also says that 43% of the women having an abortion claim to have a Protestant religious affiliation and that an additional 27% claim to be Catholic. According to their information, about 33% of women in the United States have experienced the trauma of abortion by the time they are 45 [1]. Female teens (ages 13-19) account for just under 10% of the total American female population [2], but 19% of all abortions [3].

At the PRC, I have been distraught to find that often it is Bible-believing parents who are the strongest advocates of abortion for their daughters because they are not looking at the physical, emotional, and spiritual effects of abortion in a woman's life nor are they considering the death of their grandchild. Instead they are only concerned that the family reputation be preserved and shame avoided.

A list you created in the chapter titled "The Importance of First Words" recorded aspects of your daughter's pregnancy that made you sad and that made you mad. This list may have included: broken dreams, loss of virginity, and plans put on hold.

Think now about the 'thankful' list in that same chapter. Were you able to say you're glad your daughter is healthy? Other 'thankful' aspects of her pregnancy might include: She is choosing life for her child, and she looking for ways to give birth to a healthy child. In days to come, I hope that the 'thankful' side of your list will grow to become longer than the 'sad.'

Susan found, "My daughter's grandparents, from both sides of the family, and her godparents were particularly supportive. One of her godmothers became a replacement mother to my daughter at those times when I felt that I could not go on."

Sally shares, "I remember a day when I was speaking with my daughter Lisa, early in her pregnancy. I asked Lisa why she felt she couldn't go through with her pregnancy. Lisa cried and said, 'Grandma and Grandpa are going to hate me!' I then took the liberty of sharing with her that her Grandmother was pregnant with Aunt Joan when she got married. I then mentioned other couples who had faced similar circumstances. That was a break-through day for Lisa. She settled down and accepted her pregnancy."

I have enjoyed several photos of my great-great-grandmother. Jane Maria looks solemn and proper. When I found her marriage record to Amos and compared it to the birth records for her first son, Taylor, I found there was only a two month interval. Amos had just returned from a seven month trip to Texas looking for homestead land. Obviously the farewell before the trip had been too passionate!

Though it may be tempting to hide your daughter's pregnancy, this is a time for honesty and a time to gather the support of your true friends.

Notes:
[1] "In the Know: Questions About Pregnancy, Contraception and Abortion". Guttmacher Institute. www.guttmacher.org/in-the-know/index.html accessed October 26, 2007.
[2] U.S. Census 2000 Summary File 1.
[3] "Facts on Induced Abortion In The United States." Guttmacher Institute, May 2006.

Prayer:
Dear Jesus, we thank You for friends and family in times of crisis. Most of all, we are grateful You have called us Your friend. You are a friend who sticks closer than a brother.

To Do:
Take the sin list from the chapter "The Importance of First Words" and add any further thoughts you've had. Then mark item each with either 'S' for secret or 'P' if it is publicly known.

From today's reading, what choices did David make to try to hide his sin?

Write about the following topics.
Why I won't consider abortion...

How Satan is tempting me with thoughts of abortion...

List couples or individuals you know who have conceived before marriage. What did they do? Did they choose God's way? If you don't know friends in this situation, think of Biblical accounts (like David and Bathsheba) or fictional ones (like "The Scarlet Letter," or "Les Miserables").

You might enjoy reading the book "Unspoken" by Francine Rivers, Tyndale House, 2001. It is a wonderful retelling of Bathsheba's story.

11. How Will My Church Respond?

Laugh with your happy friends when they're happy; share tears when they're down. Romans 12:15 (MES)

Suggested Reading: Romans 12:9-16   The Family of God

This is Dee's story. "I had been suspicious for some time that Lori, 15, was pregnant and asked her two or three times but she always said no. I prayed fervently, asking God to intercede. What I really wanted was for the situation to go away. I wanted to wake up one morning and find that everything was okay.

"One Sunday evening, friends invited me to attend church with them. At the end of the service, people were asked to come forward if they needed prayer. I was up and walking down the aisle before I realized what I was doing. I didn't express any particular need to the person who prayed for me.

"After the service, as I was leaving, a man ran up the aisle toward me. He said, 'God gave me a word this afternoon in prayer and I'm sure it's for you.' I had no idea who this man was. I had never seen him before.

"These are the scripture verses he handed me: Joshua 1:8-9, 'This book of the law shall not depart from your mouth, but you shall meditate on it day and night, so that you may be careful to do according to all that is written in it; for then you will make your way prosperous, and then you will have good success. Have I not commanded you? Be strong and courageous! Do not tremble, nor be dismayed, for the Lord your God is with you wherever you go.' (NASB)

"My first thought was that this was a beautiful scripture showing God's faithfulness. My second thought was 'Oh, no, God, that's not what I want to hear.' The high school guidance counselor called me and told me I needed to come to school. When I arrived I found out that Lori was indeed pregnant. I was so thankful for the Bible verses assuring me that I didn't need to be afraid or dismayed but that I could be strong and of good courage because the Lord was with me. I knew I couldn't handle it on my own."

I hope that your church fellowship will be supportive. Jean found that her church had a counselor who could deal with pregnant teenagers and their parents. The counselor was very helpful, informing them of maternity homes, pregnancy help centers, and adoption agencies who could be part of a support team. The counselor gently reminded Jean's daughter of her need to confess her sin to God and to her family. "The miracle of each unique human life was presented in such a precious way," said Jean, "I felt my life was forever changed with a new appreciation of the value of pre-born children."

Does your church have a policy about how they will handle a member's pregnancy outside of marriage? Do you know a church leader (elder, deacon, Sunday school teacher, youth group leader, small group leader) that you could meet with first so that they can go with you to talk to the pastor?

If your church is not supportive of you and your family, you will need to build your support team from other resources. In the appendix is a list of some of the pro-life offices for major denominations. I also give toll-free numbers where help is available, and websites that list pregnancy help centers. I hope that you will avail yourself of the outstanding support available at a pregnancy help center near you. I pray the Lord will bring wise counsel and sweet comfort from your local church.

Prayer:

Father God, I cast my cares and the burdens of this situation onto You. I am trusting You to sustain me and my child. I pray that our church will be part of the ministry of reconciliation to my family. Lord, I forgive my child for the wrongs that she has done and ask You to forgive me for the mistakes I may have made in parenting. I ask You to bind up and heal our broken hearts through Your Holy Spirit, through the scripture, and through the love of our church and family.

To Do:

Did the Lord give you a warning, like He gave Dee? Did you sense that something major was about to happen in your life?

Write your fears about how your church will respond to your daughter's pregnancy.

Has your church previously experienced a pregnancy in a single woman? If so, what happened?

Write the names of people you are afriad to tell as you fear judgment Pray for these individuals and groups.

Write here the names and phone numbers of those people at church to contact.

Build your support community. Make an appointment for you and your daughter at the local pregnancy resource center. Call 1-800-395-HELP to be connected with a nearby PRC. Write here the date and time of your appointment:

Call your best friend for support. Note here anything they say that is meaningful or encouraging to you today.

12. Where Is God In All Of This?

Blessed is the man who perseveres under trial, because when he has stood the test, he will receive the crown of life that God has promised to those who love him. James 1:12 (NIV)

Suggested Reading: Psalm 34:15-22   The Lord Delivers

Listen to Joy's experience. "My husband and I were surrounded with support. We were blessed to be the members of a church body which was interested in reconciliation, restoration, and healing. We received only love, compassion, and support, with not one word of criticism. One special couple contacted, on our behalf, the pastor who wrote the book 'Daddy I'm Pregnant.' He listened and tenderly encouraged us with his wise counsel.

"I do not know how those without the Lord cope with this type of crisis. We leaned on Jesus as if we were physically unable to stand. Through God's Word and His people, we made daily forward progress. There were moments of questioning why God allowed this, why He hadn't protected our daughter from her foolishness, but Jesus always reassured us that He would redeem this time and heal our wounds. We knew beyond any doubt that the Lord was in control.

"I wish I could count all of the ways the Lord has redeemed the situation, but He has been so generous with us that it is impossible to count them all. We have been blessed by the love and support of friends and family. Our daughter has recommitted her life to the Lord and is actively following Him. She volunteers at the local pregnancy resource center and speaks about her experience. She has befriended and counseled several pregnant teens and their parents. We have had many opportunities to love and encourage unwed mothers. Our greatest blessing has been our precious granddaughter."

Isn't it encouraging to note that as you are in the midst of a crisis those who have experienced the pregnancy of an unwed daughter can affirm that the Lord wants to redeem the situation and bring blessings to your family through it? What assurance we have that God hears our cries and answers our prayers. As the famous "Footsteps" poem points out, when, in our journey with the Lord, we see only one set of footsteps instead of two, that is the time the Lord picks us up and carries us in His arms. If you haven't yet felt God's presence , start specifically praying that you will be shown His plan and to receive His wisdom about the decisions that you are facing.

Prayer:

Dear Jesus, we thank You that You have heard our cries and know the entire situation. We thank You that Your grace is sufficient for us throughout this pregnancy and that You will strengthen us in times of weakness. We thank You that You are our hiding place and we can rest knowing that Your plans for us are good. Amen.

To Do:

Note the date of your prayer requests. Later, remember to return to your list to record the time and way God answered your prayers.

Journal answers to prayer so far; add new prayer requests:

Write answers to these questions.
Has there been any redemption in the situation yet? If so, what?

Is your daughter repentant?

What kinds of help is she looking for ?

What aspects of Psalm 34 touched your heart from today's reading?

Do you know any other Christians who have experienced a pregnancy outside of marriage? What blessings have they received?   What hardships have you noted?

13. Talking With My Husband

Two are better than one, because they have a good return for their work. Ecclesiastes 4:9 (NIV)

Suggested Reading: Ecclesiastes 4:9-12   Two Together

Joy stated, "When our 20-year old daughter called from her college 1500 miles from home to tell us that she was pregnant, I responded immediately with, 'No, not you. I know what you've been taught.' My husband returned home during the conversation and I had to relay to him this most difficult and unexpected news. Our feelings ranged from grief to rage and back again. We talked and cried for most of the night. At first my husband did not want our daughter to come home for the summer, but we both realized that we needed each other. For a few days we wondered if we would live through it.

"We not only lived through it, we recovered from it. My husband and I not only permitted each other to express our pain but also drew near to each other for comfort and encouragement. We cried and prayed and talked constantly, at first, but with less intensity as time passed. We determined to live one day at a time and to maintain some sense of normalcy. Our personal struggles manifested themselves differently. My husband felt as if his little girl had died. He experienced deep and lingering grief. He had trouble understanding why the Lord had not protected our daughter. At one point late in the summer, he asked me why I was not grieving. How could I just go on as if there were no pain?"

Joy explained that she was grieving but she refused to allow it to strangle her. "Just a few weeks before we learned of our daughter's pregnancy, I had taught from Philippians at a women's retreat. The truths of that book were so fresh in my mind and heart that I expected to experience joy in the midst of suffering, and I did. Looking back, we recognize that reaching out for help and accepting the help that was offered, working together to meet our daughter's needs, working to help our son cope with his anger at the violation of his sister, and resisting the temptation to place blame were essential to our survival."

Dee shares, "I made plans for the father of our daughter's baby and his family to come to our home for the evening. As I was driving home from work I began to think I would like to drive into the sunset. God quickly brought me back to reality and showed me that this would just be running away. When my husband came home I told him why Bob's parents were coming over. This was a difficult hurdle. Burt had stated several years earlier, when our daughter's classmate got pregnant, that if it ever happened to one of our girls they would be out the door. I was fearful that this would be his response now. But being faithful to God and our family, that was never Burt's response. He lead us as we discussed the situation with our family and Bob's family."

You may find the reaction of husbands and sons is different from your own. Men may focus on their loss of ability to protect their loved one from harm. It is important for us to recognize this is a major role that God has written in the heart of a man. We must allow men to express their deep grief that their role has been violated.

Be patient with your husband, as it is most likely not as easy for him to discuss his emotions as it is for you to do so. It is also important that the two of you stand together as you work through your daughter's unexpected pregnancy. Make it a practice to discuss daily any new developments concerning your daughter. Do not allow anyone or anything to divide you. Pray together each night asking the Lord to unite you as husband and wife and mother and father making decisions and encouraging your daughter for God's glory.

Prayer:

Lord Who Is There (Jehovah Shammah), I ask You to comfort and encourage us as a couple and as parents as we face the problems of our daughter's unexpected pregnancy. Help us to lean on You for the spiritual, mental, and physical strength that we need as we face this task together. Help us to bind together in Your name, that with You we will be a three-strand cord which can not be broken.

To Do:

Go back to the chapter "Hearing the Shocking News" and review the grief model.

Where in the grief cycle are you and your husband now?

Ask your husband about his pain. Does he feel he failed as a protector?

How does he identify with Joy's husband in the story above?

Are you grieving in the same way as your husband? If not, how is his response different?

How does the situation tempt you to doubt God?

How are your daughter's siblings being affected?

How can you encourage open family communication?

How do you plan to speak to the father (and his parents) of your daughter's baby?

How do you and your husband plan to support each other in this difficult time? Please agree to stand together in all discussions and decisions.

14. Who Is the Pregnant Single Mother?

For I know the plans I have for you, declares the Lord, plans to prosper you and not to harm you, plans to give you hope and a future. Then you will call upon me and come and pray to me, and I will listen to you. You will seek me and find me when you seek me with all your heart. Jeremiah 29:11-13 (NIV)

Selected Reading:
Luke 1:26-38 and Matthew 1:18-25   Birth of Jesus

When you say "unwed mother" does a stereotype leap to your mind? The American single, pregnant woman can be ANY woman. Today, more than one third of the babies conceived in the United States will be born to a young woman without a husband. She can be from any economic class, any educational group, any racial group, from a devout Christian home or a home where no faith is practiced. As mentioned in the first chapter, 69.5% of the children in the African American community are born to single mothers, as are 63.3% of children in the American Indian or Alaskan Native populations, 47.9% of children with Hispanic mothers and 25% of children with Caucasian mothers [1].

When a child gets into any behavior that is not acceptable to family morals, one of the parent's first instincts is to blame themselves. A parent will often wonder, "Did I spend enough time with my child? Was I involved enough in their lives? Did I fail to train them spiritually?" But the "what if" game is unproductive. Don't spend a lot of time beating yourself up or judging yourself harshly.

As parents, we cannot control our teens' behavior. If you look around you will see many families who have neglected and even abused their children but the young people turn out fine. Likewise, many parents who have dedicated their lives to responsibly bringing up their children find that their child choses wrong paths. If you have more than one child, you already recognize that each child is unique. Even with the same parenting and environment, children are free to respond individually. One child may be very obedient and follow the path desired by his parents, while a sibling rebels against every family value.

It is often helpful to share with a group of parents who are going through the same sorts of problems. Some pregnancy resource centers host a support group for the parents of pregnant single young women. Or perhaps your church has a small group devoted to helping parents through the teenage years. Another option is to use the Group Leader's Guide designed to accompany this book, available from Chalfont House (www. ChalfontHouse.com), and start your own small group with other parents of a pregnant Christian single.

In the United States every year more than 750,000 girls under the age of 20 become pregnant [2]. Around half of these pregnancies end in abortion. The negative social influences facing young people today are far heavier than they were when most parents were teenagers. Most common sense sexual restraints have disappeared from films, television, radio, print media, and the Internet. The advertising industry seems to sell everything with either an overt or subtle sexual message. Peer pressure can be intense. About half of the teens who graduate from high school have already engaged in premarital sex.

Despite, or maybe because of, extensive sex education, our culture has disconnected sex from pregnancy. Often the teenage girl is the one most profoundly shocked to find herself pregnant. More than likely her reaction to her pregnancy will be fear. Fear of what her parents, her boyfriend, and her friends will think of her pregnancy, fear of the changes in her body, and fear of childbirth. Our job is to help her realize pregnancy is not the end of her life or of her dreams. She does have hope and a future.

An August 2004 study by the National Center on Addiction and Substance Abuse (CASA) at Columbia University found a strong connection between teen sexual behavior and substance abuse [3]. Since your daughter has been sexually active, you should be alert to the increased probability that she has also tried alcohol, marijuana, and cigarettes. There are several resources on the Internet to help you talk to your child about smoking and alcohol/drug use. Get online, do some reading, and then schedule a frank discussion with your daughter about these substances.

Notes:

[1] National Vital Statistics Reports, Volume 55, Number 11, December 28, 2006. http://www.cdc.gov/nchs/data/nvsr/nvsr55/nvsr55_11.pdf
[2] TeenPregnancy.org, "General Facts and Stats," updated November 2006.
[3] National Center on Addiction and Substance Abuse at Columbia Univeristy, "CASA 2004 Teen Survey", www.casacolumbia.org

Prayer:

Most High God (El Elyon), in this time of turmoil, calm our hearts and give us a vision for Your plans and purposes in our life and in the lives of our daughter and grandchild. Help us to remember You are in control and that You can bring good out of any circumstance.

To Do:

What are your "what if" or "if only" thoughts?

Would it bring you peace to confess any of your perceived mistakes to the Lord and to your family? If so, consider this approach: Create a cross of wood or cardboard. Stand it up in a bowl or other container with sand or stones. Write your mistakes on small pieces of paper (sticky notes, or index cards work well) and have your family do the same for themselves. Tack the notes to the cross. Read 1 John 1:9 out loud, then remove the notes from the cross and burn or shred them. Determine to leave behind "what if" mistakes and sins and to build life anew.

With your daughter, list here all the dreams and hopes you have for her future and that she has for her future.

My hopes and dreams   Her hopes and dreams

Who Is The Pregnant Single Mother?

Read Luke 1:26-38 and Matthew 1:18-25. Mary must have felt confused when the angel Gabriel told her that she would become pregnant before marriage. She feared people would misunderstand the miracle of the virgin birth of Jesus. What verses record her emotions?

What did Joseph think?

What did Joseph plan to do?

You might enjoy reading Unafraid by Francine Rivers, Tyndale House, 2001. It is a wonderful retelling of the story of Mary.

15. What Is My Daughter Feeling?

For God did not give us a spirit of timidity, but a spirit of power, of love and of self-discipline. 2 Timothy 1:7 (NIV)

Suggested reading:　　Psalm 23　　　　　　A Shepherd's Song

The pregnant unmarried woman has many emotions raging in her mind all at once. She is probably embarrassed that people will learn she is sexually active. I have seen teenagers deny for seven months of pregnancy that they are sexually active and pregnant. In the denial which comes with this embarrassment, she may begin to wear baggy clothes, jumpers, big sweaters, and sweat suits to mask her changing body. Hopefully a sympathetic parent can help their child through this denial quickly so that she can get the medical care she needs.

She may also be fearful. Questions flood her mind. What does the future hold? Can I finish high school? Will I be able to go on to college? Will my boyfriend acknowledge that this is his child or will he deny me and the child? How will my parents react? Will they throw me out of the house? Where will I live? How will I support myself if my parents turn against me?

At the PRC we seek to determine what are the main motivators that are pushing a woman toward abortion. Fear is typically a prominent theme. Paul Swope wrote an interesting research paper about the way a woman faces an unexpected pregnancy. She sees no good choices, only three evil ones. Often the pregnancy is seen as the death of self. She may think that motherhood, adoption, and abortion all bring death, in one way or another, to her sense of self [1]. The pregnant woman perceives that the child will negate who she is and eliminate her future. Her thinking then becomes twisted to see an abortion as a self-defense mechanism. She reasons that either she or the baby must die.

In our maturity we recognize that adoption is a life affirming answer to an unexpected pregnancy. But to an uncounseled woman, adoption often appears to be a more violent act than abortion. The mother imagines a death of herself in not knowing the future of the adopted child, so she sees herself as a poor protector and a bad mother who abandons her child to an uncertain future. In my decades of counseling, I have heard many women say this exact sentence: "I would rather kill my baby than place it for adoption because at least I would know where it is." Adoption is seen as death or abandonment, and as providing no resolution.

In the midst of our disappointment and shock as parents, it's important that we calmly try to understand what the pregnant young woman is feeling. This is not a time for blaming or condemning but a time for mercy and support. Your reassurance of love and ongoing help can make a world of difference to your daughter in the midst of her turmoil. You can help her understand that her life will not end if she carries the baby to term and parents or makes a plan for adoption. When a teen's parents are involved in the girl's life, the teen is six times more likely to make a plan for adoption. When teens are asked to compare adoption to single parenting, they are also six times more likely to choose adoption [2].

Notes:
[1] Equipped to Serve. Cyndi Philkill. Frontlines, 1995.
[2] "Pro-Life Dilemma: Pregnancy Centers and the Welfare Trap." Frederica Mathewes-Green. Policy Review, July-August 1996, Number 78. http://www.policyreview.org/jul96/green.html

Prayer:
Gentle Shepherd, we thank You that You are a God of mercy and compassion. We know that You understand our fear and the fear in our daughter's heart. Help us to lean on You as we use Your power to love and to exercise self-discipline. We seek to follow You into green, peaceful pastures where our needs are met and our souls are comforted.

To Do:
Update your list of prayer requests and answers:

What Is My Daughter Feeling?

Talk with your daughter about her fears. List here some of your fears and your daughters fears.

My fears…   Her fears…

Complete the following thoughts:
I see adoption as….

My daughter sees adoption as….

I see parenting as…

My daughter sees parenting as…

I see abortion as….

My daughter sees abortion as…

Make a comparison chart of the advantages and disadvantages:

Adoption   Single Parenting   Married Parenting   Abortion

How can you help and encourage your daughter toward an adoption plan or a parenting plan?

16. Where Does The Baby's Father Belong In All This?

You've always been right there for me; don't turn your back on me now. Don't throw me out, don't abandon me; you've always kept the door open. My father and mother walked out and left me but God took me in. Psalm 27:9-10 (MES)

Suggested reading: Genesis 38:6-30   Judah and Tamar

We don't often put much emphasis on the father of the unexpected baby. In today's pregnancy care centers we are recognizing more and more the importance of ministry to these young men. See if your PRC can provide education and counseling to the baby's father, if he will be involved in the pregnancy and the life of your grandchild. A survey by The National Fatherhood Initiative found that 91% of respondants agreed that there is a father-absence crisis in America.   In addition, only slightly more than half of the fathers surveyed agreed that they felt adequately prepared for fatherhood when they first became fathers [1].

The young men involved in an unwed pregnancy are as unique as the pregnant young women and reflect a cross-section of the population. The young man often will experience the same fear and panic the woman feels. He, too, sees his future changed and threatened.

If the young lady carries the baby to term, he is financially responsible for the child for 18 years. The financial commitment alone is enough to cause most boys to encourage (or try to force) the girl into an abortion. Of the girls who have an abortion, a large majority say the father of the child insisted on abortion. Often he will tell her that unless she has an abortion, he's finished with her. The sad truth for a young woman who complies with his threat is that most of the relationships do not survive the abortion experience .

Some young men deny they are the father of the child. They might even recruit friends to claim that they also have had sexual relationships with the girl. With modern DNA testing, the father of the child can be determined within a few weeks of the child's birth. Your doctor can refer you to a local facility and you can research facilities and procedures by searching the Internet. Consult with your doctor before using any service.

Although paternity DNA procedures can be used before birth, it is not recommended due to the increased risk of infection, miscarriage, or trauma. For example, Chorionic Villi Sampling (CVS) tests can be used at 11-13 weeks of gestation. For this procedure, a sample of the placenta is compared to a blood sample or mouth swab from mother and the alleged father. CVS has a slightly higher risk of miscarriage than amniocentesis.

Amniocentesis paternity testing is generally performed between 14-20 weeks of pregnancy. Fetal cells in the amniotic fluid are compared to a blood sample or mouth swab from the mother and the alleged father.

I recommend that you wait until the baby is born so that a comparison of blood samples between the baby and the alleged father can be made more safely. The baby's DNA can easily be collected with a swab of the cheek cells or blood from the umbilical cord.

In all cases, talk to your OBGYN about each course of action. Ask about the possible complications and the frequency with which each occurs. You may even wish to speak with several different doctors. There is also quite a bit of information on the Internet about paternity testing. Do your research, ask questions, and pray about what course to take.

Parents can face pain as they think of their grandchild's father. Jean writes, "I was very bitter because of his response to it all: flight. One day I accidentally ran into him. He was so embarrassed that he could not make eye contact with me. I was filled with an intense sadness at his loss. He was walking away from one who would have been a faithful lifemate and from this beautiful gift from God – his son."

Some young men will step up to the plate and suggest that they get married. We will talk about marriage later in this book. Other men will state that though they don't see marriage at this time, they would like to be a support to the girl throughout the pregnancy. It can be very helpful to a pregnant young woman to have this emotional support if the relationship is deemed to be a productive and solid friendship. When possible, I think it is important for the parents of pregnant teenagers to meet face to face to examine the future and decide how to support the new mother.

The CASA 2004 Teen Survey [2] found that "girls with boyfriends 2 or more years older are more than twice as likely to drink; almost six times likelier to get drunk; six times likelier to have tried marijuana; and 4.5 times likelier to smoke than girls whose boyfriends are less than 2 years older or who do not have a boyfriend." The same survey also found that "teens who spend 25 or more hours a week with a boyfriend/girlfriend are 2.5 times likelier to drink; 5 times likelier to get drunk; 4.5 times likelier to have tried marijuana; and more than 2.5 times likelier to smoke than those who spend less than 10 hours per week with a boyfriend or girlfriend." Talk to your daughter about these issues regardless of the age difference between her and the father of her child.

It is important to determine from the onset the level of involvement that can be expected or is desired from the father of the baby. Obviously, if your daughter was preyed upon, either through rape or coercion, there will be no necessity to involve him in your plans for the child. In Appendix A you will see a list of laws enacted in most states that protect a parent's authority over a minor child. If you feel that the young man involved in your daughter's pregnancy is a threat, you could pursue a restraining order with the police. Other ways to protect your daughter include sending her to live with a relative or other close friend and sending her to live in a maternity home.

If the young man is merely a casual acquaintance of your daughter, discuss with a pastor, lawyer, or counselor whether or not he should be involved with your daughter. It may be tempting to exclude the father entirely, but remember to make an adoption plan for the child, both the mother and father must relinquish their parental rights. The child's father has rights and he can go to court to get visitation or guardianship. No paternal rights can be signed away until after the birth of the child. Check with your adoption attorney or agency for the laws of your state.

If the young man is a long-term friend of your daughter, arrange a meeting with him, his parents, and possibly a neutral observer. During this discussion, resist the urge to place blame or to lecture. Rather, listen and hear his views of the situation. Verbally express to the young man and his family your forgiveness and your desire to support your daughter throughout the pregnancy and for the future.

Notes:

[1] National Fatherhood Initiative. "Pop's Culture: A National Survey of Dads' Attitudes on Fathering." 2006. www.fatherhood.org

[2] National Center on Addiction and Substance Abuse at Columbia Univeristy, "CASA 2004 Teen Survey", www.casacolumbia.org

Prayer:

Dear God who sees everything (El Roi), we pray that You will be working in the heart of our grandchild's father. We ask that he will treat our daughter with respect, and will support her. We pray that he will take seriously his fatherhood responsibilities. Give us grace and forgiveness as we work with him for our daughter's and grandchild's best future. Help us to see clearly and trust You, for You know the beginning, middle, and end of our situation.

To Do:

You might enjoy reading the book Unveiled by Francine Rivers, 2001, Tyndale. It is a wonderful version of the story of Tamar.

What I learned from the story of Judah and Tamar (Genesis 38):

How did Judah and his sons fail Tamar?

Where Does The Baby's Father Belong?

What was Tamar's solution to their failure?

What did Judah say of Tamar?

Why do you think God included Tamar in the lineage of Christ?

How does Tamar's story speak to your situation?

In conversation with your daughter, find out where she thinks the relationship with the baby's father will be in five years. Write about her thoughts here:

How much time per week does your daughter spend with the father of her child now?

How much time did she spend with him per week before she was pregnant?

Write about the factors in their relationship, including: their ages, level of schooling completed, and the suitability of the relationship.

Sketch the character of the father of your grandchild by answering the following questions:

Who is he morally and spiritually? (Examples: He is actively involved in a church similar to our own; his values reflect ours; he was only interested in sex and has abandoned our daughter; he is driving our daughter away from us.)

What kind of family does he come from? (Examples: Is it a strong or weak family? Are his parents married to each other?)

What is his commitment level to your daughter? (Examples: He wants to marry our daughter; our daughter is one of several of his girlfriends)

What are the prospects for his future? (Examples: Is he a good student? Is he a hard worker? What education and job skills does he possess?)

17. Forgiving The Baby's Father

Therefore be clear minded and self-controlled so that you can pray. Above all, love each other deeply, because love covers over a multitude of sins. 1 Peter 4:7b-8 (NIV)

Suggested Reading: Colossians 3:12-17   Christian Living

"Forgiving the father of our daughter's child was difficult," says Joy, "because he was not involved in his daughter's life. We had not met him and we were able to avoid the issue of forgiveness toward him. I found myself feeling self-righteous in my anger because he rejected my daughter and granddaughter when they needed him."

As a Christian, you can't indefinitely avoid the topic of forgiving the child's father. We are commanded to forgive, and Jesus says that unforgiveness interferes with our spiritual life and our prayers. Of course it can be hard to forgive, but its better to start working on forgiveness sooner rather than later. Unforgiveness will eat YOU up inside.

Remember forgiveness is not an option. Jesus commands us to forgive, warning us that we will be forgiven as we forgive (Matthew 6:14-15). Two quotes that I like on forgiveness are, "Unforgiveness is the only poison you swallow hoping it will kill the other person" (source unknown); and "Forgiveness does not mean condoning what has been done. Forgiving means abandoning your right to pay back the perpetrator in his own coin, but it is a loss that liberates the victim" (Bishop Desmond Tutu).

What exactly is forgiveness? Philosopher Joanna North says forgiveness is when we decide to "view the wrongdoer with compassion, benevolence, and love while recognizing that he has willfully abandoned" us [1]. Social researcher C.T. Coyle defines forgiveness as "the conscious decision to withhold both retribution and resentment and to instead offer mercy to the undeserving offender" [2]. Dr. Enright says, "When the forgiver gives up his justified resentment and his right to retaliate, he is giving the offender a gift she doesn't deserve and, as he does so, he receives a gift himself, the gift of healing. So forgiveness benefits both the forgiver and the one forgiven" [3].

Forgiveness should not be confused with excusing, pardoning, forgetting, or reconciliation. God did not design us to be able to forget instantly or easily. Remembering is how we learn, how we may avoid making the same mistake over and over. While you may eventually forget any offense, you can still forgive whether or not you ever forget. Lewis Smedes says that "forgetting, in fact, may be a dangerous way to escape the inner surgery of the heart that we call forgiving" [4]. So forgetting is not the same as forgiving.

Forgiveness is also not the same as excusing. When an offender is excused for their wrongdoing, the excuser must have a rational reason for deciding that the offender cannot be held responsible. If the offender cannot be held responsible, then there is no offense to forgive. Forgiveness is not the same as pardoning. To pardon an offender is to relase them from the penalties they deserve. We can forgive someone whether or not they ever suffer any penalites.

Forgiveness does not demand reconciliation in the relationship. Reconciliation depends on trust. You can forgive someone without trusting them and without necessarily resuming a relationship with them. Forgiveness can even occur without ever receiving an apology or a recognition of wrongdoing from the offender.

Forgiveness may not be a one-time act on your part. Matthew 18:21-22 says, "Then Peter came and said to Him, 'Lord, how often shall my brother sin against me and I forgive him? Up to seven times?' Jesus said to him, 'I do not say to you, up to seven times, but up to seventy times seven.'" These verses point out that forgiveness is to be an on-going activity in your spirit. Forgiveness of others frees you from the past, frees you to forgive yourself, frees you to heal and grow, and creates dignity for all parties involved.

Finally, forgivness is a decision, not a feeling. Don't be surprised if it takes time to feel forgiving towards yourself and others. Decide to start changing your thoughts about the ones who need to be forgiven. As your thoughts change, your behavior will start to change. As behavior changes, your feelings will begin to change. So begin now to think forgiving thoughts. Next, start to act in a forgiving way, and then you will begin to feel the forgiveness.

Notes:

[1] North, Joanna. "Wrongdoing and Forgiveness," *Philosophy*, 62, 1987, pp. 499-508.
[2] Coyle, C.T. "Men and Abortion: A Path to Healing." Life Cycle Books, 1999.
[3] Enright, R.D., and the Human Development Study Group. "Counseling Within the Forgiveness Triad: On Forgiving, Receiving Forgiveness, and Self-forgiveness," *Counseling and Values*, 40, 1996, pp. 107-146.
[4] Smedes, Lewis. "Forgive and Forget: Healing the Hurts We Don't Deserve." HarperOne. 2007.

Prayer:

Dear Lord, help us to stay in a right relationship with You by forgiving everyone involved in this unexpected pregnancy. Grant us peace, enable us to work together for the benefit of our daughter, the young man, and our grandchild. I pray that You will give me the power to treat them well and to be merciful, kind and compassionate to them, just as You are. I thank You for Your kindness in forgiving me. I accept Your forgiveness and will extend it to others in the name of Jesus.

To Do:

From today's reading in Colossians 3:12-17, what qualities should you clothe yourself in?

What do you learn about forgiveness in the following verses?
Psalm 86:5 "For You, Lord, are good, and ready to forgive, and abundant in lovingkindness to all who call upon You."

1 John 1:9 "If we confess our sins, He is faithful and righteous to forgive us our sins and to cleanse us from all unrighteousness."

Micah 7:18 "Who is a God like you, who pardons sin and forgives the transgression of the remnant of his inheritance? You do not stay angry forever but delight to show mercy."

2 Chronicles 7:14 "[If] My people who are called by My name humble themselves and pray and seek my face and turn from their wicked ways, then I will hear from heaven, will forgive their sin and heal their land."

Mark 11:25 "And when you stand praying, if you hold anything against anyone, forgive him, so that your Father in heaven may forgive you."

Matthew 6:14-15 "For if you forgive others for their transgressions, your heavenly Father will also forgive you. But if you do not forgive others, then your Father will not forgive your transgressions."

Make a list of songs of thankfulness (Examples: Amazing Grace; How Can I Give Thanks)

Make a list of songs about the fruits that should be in our lives (Example: It Is Well With My Soul)

Create an artistic expression of your praise to God: a dance, painting, needlework, or song, etc.

Write a note of forgiveness to the baby's father. This note should NOT be sent, just recorded here.

18. Forgiving The Young Man's Parents

Do not be anxious about anything, but in everything, by prayer and petition, with thanksgiving, present your requests to God. And the peace of God, which transcends all understanding, will guard your hearts and your minds in Christ Jesus. Philippians 4:6-7 (NIV)

Suggested Reading: Philippians 4:4-9   God's Peace

Just as daughters fear their parents' reaction to an unexpected pregnancy, young men often feel the same fear. If the baby's father is an adult, he may not even notify his parents about the pregnancy. If he is a teenager, he also may desire to keep his parents ignorant about the expected birth of the child. I have seen young men promise to relinquish parental rights and visitation if his parents are not informed that he has fathered a child. One young man, terrified of his single mother's reaction to his girlfriend's pregnancy, kept crying out, "It was only sex! It was only sex!" Too often our media has disconnected sex from pregnancy!

Kay says, "It is so easy to think that your daughter would have acted according to the principles she had been taught if only the boy had been properly raised. But the blame game is a dead end street. Once I met my daughter's boyfriend's parents, I recognized they had the same hopes and desires for their son as I had for my daughter. They were just as anguished by the pregnancy as I was. Rather than blame each other, we found the best solution was to work together to support our children. When all of us adults took responsibility for our own failures while forgiving each other, we were able to provide a positive example to our children to do the same."

I have encountered a few cases in which the young man's parents have wanted to become extremely involved in the pregnancy, even to the point of seeking to adopt the child for themselves or one of their family members. This can be problematic because the pregnant young woman may be treated as merely a vehicle to deliver a much-wanted child, with her feelings and desires being steamrolled by the agenda of the young man's parents. It may be necessary to contact a lawyer to notify the parents that grandparents have no standing in court on the matters concerning the child of their son or daughter.

I hope the young man involved with your daughter is a vulnerable and caring person whose parents will also be concerned for your daughter's well being. Obviously it is best when all the parties involved are mature and caring.

Review the information about forgiveness in the previous chapter about forgiving the baby's father, then read these principles found in the acrostic FORGIVE, below:

F – Forgive the hurt done to you. Matthew 6:14-15 (NIV) – If you forgive men when they sin against you, your heavenly father will also forgive you. But if you do not forgive men their sins, your father will not forgive your sins.

O – Offer up your confession to Jesus for your own sins. 1 John 1:9 (NIV) – If we confess our sins, He is faithful and just and will forgive us our sins and purify us from all unrighteousness.

R – Recognize the people you have hurt. Matthew 5:23-24 (NIV) – Therefore, if you are offering your gift at the altar, and there remember that your brother has something against you, leave your gift there in front of the altar, first go and be reconciled with your brother; then come and offer your gift.

G – Give active love and blessings to those you are forgiving. Romans 12:17-21 (NIV) – Do not repay anyone evil for evil. Be careful to do what is right in the eyes of everybody. If it is possible, as far as it depends on you, live at peace with everyone. Do not take revenge, my friends, but leave room for God's wrath for it is written: 'It is mine to avenge; I will repay,' said the Lord. On the contrary: 'If your enemy is hungry, feed him; if he is thirsty, give him something to drink. In doing this, you will be heaping coals of fire upon his head.' Do not be overcome by evil but overcome evil with good.

I – Implore God to bless those you have hurt. Matthew 5:44-48 (NIV) – But I tell you: love your enemies and pray for those who persecute you, that you may be sons of your father in heaven. He causes his sun to rise on the evil and the good, and he sends rain on the righteous and the unrighteous. If you love those who love you, what reward will you get? Are not even the tax collectors doing that? And if you greet only your brothers, what are you doing more than others? Do not even pagans do that? Be perfect, therefore, as your heavenly father is perfect.

V – Value, in prayer, your enemies believing Jesus can change them. Romans 14:4 (NIV) – Who are you to judge someone else's servant? To his own master he stands or falls and he will stand, for the Lord is able to make him stand.

E – Embrace God's forgiveness of you with rejoicing. Ephesians 4:31-32 (NIV) – Get rid of all bitterness, rage and anger, brawling and slander, along with every form of malice. Be kind and compassionate to one another, forgiving each other, just as in Christ God forgave you.

Prayer:
Heavenly Father, grant us Your peace as together we focus on Your will. Help us to remember how much and how many times You have forgiven each of us. Make our hearts tender to You and to each other as we plan for the future.

To Do:
With your whole family, review the Forgiveness acrostic in this chapter. Invite the young man and his parents to this discussion if you think it would be helpful.

Let everyone share how they have appreciated being forgiven at some point in the past. Record some of those thoughts here:

Spend time listening to the perspectives and goals of the young man's parents. Make joint plans, if possible, for the future of your children and your grandchild. Pray together that God will be glorified in the midst of this crisis. Record some of these thoughts here:

Share your prayer requests and answers. Add new requests from the family:

Pray together for God to be glorified in this pregnancy. Close by singing a favorite hymn or song of praise together.

19. Sharing With Family And Friends

If one part suffers, every part suffers with it; if one part is honored, every part rejoices with it. 1 Corinthians 12:26 (NIV)

Suggested Reading: Psalm 84   Dwelling in God's House

It is helpful to sit down with your daughter and make a list of people that she wants to tell about her pregnancy. This list could have three parts:

First, decide on those who should be told early in the pregnancy. This list might include: your pastor (or other person with whom you feel a true spiritual connection), the baby's father and his parents, immediate family members, and supportive friends of the family. I recommend that you and your daughter speak to these people face-to-face (if they live nearby). Hopefully your daughter will receive love and acceptance from this group of friends not only through their words but also thorough hugs and body language. Be aware that there will most likely be tears, and perhaps some anger.

Siblings should be among the first to be told of their sister's pregnancy. You do not want them to hear about it from someone else. Her brothers and sisters will likely show some anger. They may be embarrassed that their sister is sexually active. They may be disappointed that she has broken God's laws and disregarded the family's values. They may also be jealous of the attention pregnancy will bring her. As time progresses, siblings may hear gossip or be isolated from others in reaction to their sister's pregnancy. I have seen youth group parents refuse to allow the siblings of a pregnant teen to date their children, fearing that sexual behavior will be repeated. This unfair condemnation can have detrimental effects on the sibling who is not sexually active. You may wish to talk to the youth leader and to the parents of your teen's friends, asking them to be prayerfully supportive of your entire family.

Second, after the first three months of pregnancy, you may wish to notify her school counselor and selected teachers if the pregnancy will be visible before the school year is completed. At this time, sit down with your pastor and discuss when to tell your church's ruling body and Sunday School teachers. Your daughter may contact these people by phone or email. Sit with her while she places any calls. Allow your daughter the responsibility and privilege of making these calls.

Third, near the end of the second trimester (about the fifth month), your daughter's pregnancy will begin to be noticeable. Now would be a good time to tell relatives who do not live nearby and anyone else who hasn't yet been told. This group of people could be contacted through a form letter you and your daughter write together, giving as much or as little information as she desires.

Ask all the above groups for their prayers and thoughtful support. Suggest that they send encouraging notes or small gifts (a single item of maternity clothing, for example), give a cheerful phone call, or invite your daughter to participate in an activity she enjoys.

I do not recommend that you try to create a "family secret" around your daughter's pregnancy if she chooses to make an adoption plan for the baby. Though it may be tempting, family secrets are not beneficial because they foster shame and fear of discovery. These fears eat away at the emotional and relational health of the family. In addition, secrecy sends a message of shame and rejection to your daughter at a time when she most needs loving support and acceptance. With open adoption she will be able to know about her child and may even visit from time to time, so secrecy may not even be possible.

As you tell people about your daughter's pregnancy, be prepared for a torrent of advice about what should be done. You will find strong feelings for all options: for abortion, for single-parenting, for adoption, and even for a quick wedding. Explain that your daughter and her child are loved, valued, and you trust your daughter to make the best decision she can regarding this child.

Family members who live in other areas may suggest that your daughter come to live with them during her pregnancy in order to avoid unpleasantness in her school or youth group. You can discuss in private the options presented and then unite as a family to support her as she acts on her decisions.

It is important for your entire family to have a strong network of support. Hopefully the people you contact will form this solid core of support.

Prayer:
Faithful Guide, please guide us as we decide whom to contact at various times. We pray that You will prepare the hearts of those we love with mercy, understanding, love, and support for our family and our daughter.

To Do:
Write a list of people to tell now, and those to tell in future months.
Tell Now   Tell Later

With your daughter, write out a phone script for the first people she will contact:

Write a template letter with your daughter that will be used to notify people later in the pregnancy. Perhaps something like this: Dear _____, our daughter _____ (name) will have a baby on about _____ (date). At thist time she is planning to parent/make an adoption plan. We covet your prayers and expressions of support. Yours,

_____

Sit with your daughter as she makes calls or writes letters.

With your spouse, talk privately with each of your other children. Explain the situation according to the age and maturity of the child. Ask for their support. Listen to their ideas, emotions, and fears. Pray with them. How did these conversations go?

Have a family meeting of support for your pregnant daughter. What support can each member of the family give?

110

Continue to take time with each child. Write here how you plan to do this. What special things do you plan for each child?

Journal about today's reading in Psalm 84:
Draw a picture, or write a poem, about being a nesting bird in God's house.

Draw a picture of God's home or create a collage of pictures from magazines (you may need to use a separate sheet of paper).

The "Valley of Baca" can be translated "Valley of Tears." How will you use your tears to refresh others?

20. Forgiving Myself

The Lord is compassionate and gracious, slow to anger, abounding in love. Psalm 103:8 (NIV)

Suggested Reading: Psalm 103   Bless the Lord

No matter what your home life is like, you are not to blame for your daughter's pregnancy. It is common for parents to feel that they have failed to give their daughter adequate training in spiritual and moral issues. You may also feel that you didn't supervise your daughter with enough scrutiny. Hindsight is 20/20.

If the Lord convicts you of something in your relationship with your daughter, ask the Lord to forgive you. Talk to your daughter privately: confess the sin and ask her forgiveness. Remind your daughter that even as she has made bad choices, so have you. It may be helpful to share with her some of your own past mistakes and what you did to remedy the situations your sin created.

As a parent you need to stay close to your spouse. This is not a time to blame each other for the situation. This is a time for family unity. All children need to see that their parents really love and support each other. In crisis, children need to recognize that their parents are a team. Don't allow the crisis to divert all of your attention to your pregnant daughter. Work at building your marriage. Deliberately take time to talk to your spouse about your thoughts and fears.

To forgive yourself may take some effort. Avoid the traps of focusing on placing blame, of endlessly wondering "what if..", or of negative self-talk. Maintain your regular activities, resist the temptation to hide at home and sink into depression. When you catch yourself thinking unforgiving thoughts toward yourself, stop and breathe. Then pray and ask the Lord to remove your negative thoughts. Your daughter will need a lot of your time and energy, but schedule time with your other children too. Tell all your children several times a day that you love them and value them.

Bless them with words of encouragement. Spend time journaling your thoughts and emotions.

Winston Churchill was famous for his admonition of encouragement to the British people during the bombing of London in World War II: "Never give up! Never give up! Never give up!" God is present in the midst of your crisis. He has a plan that will result in hope and a future for you, your daughter, her child, and your family.

Prayer:
Faithful Father, we thank You that You are a God noted for Your faithfulness through the generations. Help us to cling to You as we forgive ourselves and those around us by imitating Your example of love.

To Do:
Talk openly with your daughter about bad choices you have each made. How did this conversation go?

Draw a picture of what "never give up" means. (Have you seen the cartoon of the heron who is trying to swallow a frog head-first? The frog's hands are sticking out of the heron's beak. The frog is clasping the heron's neck, closing the throat so that he can't be swallowed.)

Make a list of what you are doing to build up your marriage.

What are you doing to build your relationship with your kids, with your friends, and with God?

Write about ways to acknowledge you have missed God's target. Refer to Romans 3:23, Romans 5:17-18, and Romans 14:4.

How do you see God in the midst of this crisis?

From today's reading in Psalm 103, write about the character of God.

Write and send a thank you note to someone who has been encouraging to you, your daughter, or your family.

21. Forgiving My Daughter

If you forgive men when they sin against you, your heavenly Father will also forgive you. Matthew 6:14 (NIV)

Suggested Reading: Matthew 6:9-15   The Lord's Prayer for His Disciples

As a parent in pain, it may be very difficult to face the fact that you blame your daughter for the crisis facing your family. She may indeed have rebelliously become involved in an illicit sexual relationship but don't immediately jump into that assumption. I have found that some pregnant young women are as shocked and surprised by their pregnancy as their parents. Most girls do not deliberately set out to become pregnant, though a few girls do. Despite our open discussions about sex in school and in the media, pregnancy is generally not mentioned.

Our children have been bombarded for years with unrealistic propaganda that sex and pregnancy are not connected. A 2005 survey of television [1] reviewed thousands of hours of programming containing sexual situations and determined how many of them included any reference to abstinence, contraception, waiting to have sex, or the consequences of sex. Only 14% of all shows and 11% of network prime-time shows with any sexual content include a scene with a reference to sexual risks or responsibilities. Two-thirds of all references to sexual risks or responsibilities on TV are "minor or inconsequential." Though God intended sex in marriage to be both for procreation and recreation, our culture advertises sex as a recreational activity with no unpleasant consequences.

Pregnancy is not the time to lecture or preach at your child. This is the time to listen. If your daughter is willing to talk, listen without interruption. It is important to hear what she feels should be done and how she wants to proceed. As you listen to her story, don't be afraid to put your arm around her or let her cry on your shoulder. Touch can be healing. Do a mental checklist to ensure that your words are of healing, comfort, and encouragement. Remember there is not a parent on earth who has not suffered because of something their child has done. Billy Graham comforted his friend, Roger Palms, and Palms states, "My friend listened carefully, perhaps remembering his own struggles with his son, Franklin. Then he turned to me and said, 'Always love them; never give up.'" [2]

Jesus gives us no wiggle-room when it comes to forgiveness. Matthew 5:43-48 is clear, "You have it heard that it was said, 'Love your neighbor and hate your enemy.' But I tell you: Love your enemies and pray for those who persecute you, that you may be sons of your Father in heaven. He causes his sun to rise on the evil and the good, and sends rain on the righteous and the unrighteous. If you love those who love you, what reward will you get? Are not even tax collectors doing that? And if you greet only your brothers, what are you doing more than others? Do not the pagans do that? Be perfect, therefore, as your heavenly Father is perfect."

Jesus' call is to forgive enemies and strangers. It takes no imagination to know that He also wants us to forgive those dearest to us, those who are part of our family of love.

Fear of family, fear of anger, and fear of unforgiveness are reasons many Christian girls feel they must have an abortion. It is through our true loving forgiveness that we affirm our daughters and their children. This allows them to acknowledge their sin before their Heavenly Father and repent.

Notes:
[1] "Sex on TV-4," A Kaiser Family Foundation Report, Executive Summary. 2005. www.kff.org
[2] Roger C. Palms. Pastor's family. A magazine by Focus on the Family. December 1998 – January 1999. p14-16.

Prayer:
Dear Lord, help us to show our daughter the mercy, forgiveness, and love You bestow upon us again and again in Christ Jesus.

To Do:
Is your daughter repentant?

What is she changing in her lifestyle?

How is she willing to be held accountable?

Read the Lord's Prayer in several versions of the Bible. Write the Lord's Prayer in your own words, customized to your current situation:

Review the information on forgiveness in the chapter titled "Forgiving The Baby's Father." Finish these sentences:
"I forgive my daughter for ..."

"I show my forgiveness by …"

"I need forgiveness for..."

22. Forgiving Unkind Acquaintances

Be filled with the spirit. Speak to one another with psalms, hymns, and spiritual songs. Sing and make music in your heart to the Lord, always giving thanks to God the Father for everything in the name of our Lord Jesus Christ. Ephesians 5:18b-20 (NIV)

Suggested Reading: Ephesians 5:1-21   Walking with Jesus

Will there be people of your acquaintance at church, job, or in the community who will gossip? Unfortunately, the answer is probably 'yes' for all of those groups. You and your daughter may be wounded by gossip at some point during the nine months of her pregnancy. This is not the first or last time either of you will experience hurt from others. It is another opportunity for you to practice forgiveness. Be sure you provide a safe environment for your daughter and are open and honest in your communications with her.

Assure all your children that you are parents for the long haul and will love them for their entire lives. Acknowledge to your daughter again that she is accountable to God for her behavior. Remind her of God's love and forgiveness. The great assurance we have in 1 John 1:9 is, "If we confess our sins, He is faithful and just and will forgive us our sins and purify us from all unrighteousness." Your daughter may need to be reminded daily during episodes of backbiting that she is forgiven and loved. Deuteronomy 33:27 reminds us that the "Eternal God is your refuge, and underneath are the everlasting arms." Can you picture this protection?

Prayer:
Dear Hiding Place,
We ask You to silence those who bring messages of discouragement and condemnation. Help us to forgive them and keep our eyes on You. We are grateful for Your unfailing love.

To Do:

Send notes to your daughter and to friends who are a help. Check for encouraging note cards at a Christian bookstore.

Check out www.dayspring.com for e-cards. Look under the sections for "Expecting Baby" and "Encouragement".

Go to an office supply store and make color copies of photos of your daughter growing up. Cut them out and make a special memory book for her with encouraging stories from her life. I like to buy the small 5x7 photo albums. I put a verse or message on one side and a photo or picture facing it.

23. Beauty From Ashes

Provide for those who grieve in Zion – to bestow on them a crown of beauty instead of ashes, the oil of gladness instead of mourning, a garment of praise instead of a spirit of despair. They will be called oaks of righteousness, a planting of the Lord, for the display of his splendor. Isaiah 61:3 (NIV)

Suggested Reading: Isaiah 61   Joy for Sorrow

The Lord desires to use this time of trouble for your maturity. He desires to give you a heart that is sensitive to others who grieve. As you read Isaiah 61, note the many symbols God uses to show new life and a future full of hope. Like the German saying "from little acorns come mighty oaks" God will take this current acorn of trouble and grow it into a mighty oak to shelter others in their time of trouble.

Marilyn says, "I had prayed for years that my rebellious daughter would 'see the light' and return to God. Just when it looked like God was beginning to reach her and she was consciously taking steps to change her lifestyle, I was hit with the news that she was pregnant. And not only pregnant but on the verge of breaking up with her boyfriend - the one boyfriend of whom I really approved. What had looked like a step forward now seemed to be a giant step backward.

"But God was not defeated! This was His way of bringing my daughter to an abrupt change and turn her onto the path He wanted for her. She and the child's father put their own fears and interests behind, and chose to do the best for their baby. They finally chose to marry and raise the baby themselves. As they made this choice, there was a transformation in their lives that was amazing to behold - a change that was greater than I had dared to ask from God. And the precious baby, when born, was such a joyful child that she brought delight to all around her. In fact, God used that child not only to bring peace, healing, and direction to her parents but to other family members who joined in supporting and loving her. We all learned that God can truly turn ashes into beauty."

Earlier we looked at the grief / trauma model and saw that acceptance is the step before resolution of the problem. Are you step by step reaching areas of acceptance and resolution? Are you finding that you cycle through some emotional grief stages more than once? Be gentle with yourself - this is normal and to be expected.

Prayer:

Lord Who Heals (Jehovah Rapha), help us to have our eyes opened to the beauty around us. So often we are conscious only of the ashes. May we see our present circumstances through Your eyes. We ask You to bring healing in our lives.

To Do:

As I have faced the problem of pain in a Christian's life, some of the books I have enjoyed reading include: Affliction by Edith Schaeffer; When God Doesn't Make Sense by James Dobson; and Don't Waste Your Sorrows by Paul Billheimer.

List ways to turn your resignation into acceptance:

Under 'Ashes' write your despairs, your disappointments, and your feelings of abandonment by God. Under 'Beauty,' note the times and ways God has met you in the midst of your sorrow. Note the practical acts of love you have experienced from those around you.

Ashes   Beauty

What does acceptance of your daughter's pregnancy mean to you?

Below, or on a separate sheet, illustrate Isaiah 61 by drawing or creating a collage of magazine pictures.

What are symbols of new life for you?

What would your garment of praise look like? Draw it or describe it:

24. Should They Marry?

Though one may be overpowered, two can defend themselves. A chord of three strands is not quickly broken. Ecclesiastes 4:12 (NIV)

Suggested Reading: Ecclesiastes 4:9-12   The Power of Two

There are many things to consider when thinking about marriage for a young couple. Perhaps the most important issue to consider is whether the couple has the full emotional and spiritual support of both families to help them grow mature as individuals, as a married couple, and as parents. Perhaps your own parents did not have an inspirational marriage, or you have not experienced one either. Even with these challenging backgrounds, prayerfully consider whether your daughter could have a rewarding marriage of her own with the baby's father. If the couple has adequate support, almost any obstacle can be surmounted (Philippians 4:13).

Teen marriages generally have a bad reputation as leading to a guaranteed divorce. However, this reputation is not based completely on the facts. Data from the 2002 National Survey on Family Growth [1] shows that only 48% of first marriages by girls under 18 years old have dissolved by the 10th anniversary, meaning that 52% of young teen (under the age of 18) marriages were still intact after 10 years! To balance the fact that waiting until the age of 23 to marry improves the chance of the marriage lasting 10 years, we have the fact that women who bear a child without marrying have a 40% lower likelihood of *ever* marrying [2]. In addition, "marrying before the birth of a child may lead to greater paternal support, even if the marriage doesn't last. If couples marry, the male partner is likely to be a resident parent and have greater access to the child. Even if the couple eventually divorces, this early contact may lead to greater levels of financial support from the father" [3]. On the other hand, married teens are statistically more likely to have a second child relatively quickly, which may impact the mother's ability to finish her schooling.

What about not marrying, but cohabiting with the baby's father? Many studies have shown than premarital cohabitation negatively impacts both marriage and divorce [1]. Women who never cohabited are less likely to experience the dissolution of their first marriage. Only about one-third of women marry their cohabiting partner and keep the marriage intact. Another one-third of women leave that relationship without ever marrying him, and about 20% marry their cohabiting partner but later divorce. Some parents ask the teenage mother to leave home because they feel she is a bad example to her siblings. Careful thought should be exercised before asking your daughter to leave home. This can force the young mother into living with a man who, more than likely, has little interest in her baby and may even be abusive. The newspapers are full of stories about children abused or killed by their mother's boyfriend. In addition to being outside of God's plan, living together does not improve the chances that the couple will marry, nor that they will stay married.

With strong encouragement and practical support from both families, marriage can bring many benefits. Benefits to the young mother and father include:

· They have the dignity of being married. They have been affirmed by the fellow parent as being desirable for a permanent relationship.

· Their self-esteem is heightened.

· They have help caring for the child.

· They have help with the chores of homemaking.

· They have companionship.

· They have an affirming sexual relationship.

· They receive the benefits of having one home instead of two.

· They can be assured their child is benefiting.

· They will be happier, healthier, and have longer lives because they are married. The median annual income of parents in an intact first marriage is $41,000. By contrast, the annual median income of cohabiting couples with children is $33,000, and the annual median income of never-married mothers is only $15,000 [4].

· "Mothers with children who have married at some point (including those who are currently married, or are separated or divorced) are half as likely to experience domestic violence by an intimate as compared to mothers who have never been married [4].

Benefits to the child include:

· The child will know the identity of its father. The child will have a mother and a father. This will help guarantee a normal, healthy development.

· The child will share a common family name. The child will be a legal part of two family trees with grandparents and other extended family. The child will have a sense of rootedness that can't be destroyed even if there is later a divorce.

· The legal tie will guarantee the child will have more support even if the parents divorce. While only 48% of never-married women receive child support, more than 64.6% of divorced women do [5].

· The child is far less likely to live in poverty. "A child born and raised outside of marriage will spend an average of 51% of his childhood in poverty. By contrast, a child born and raised by both parents in an intact marriage will spend on average on 7% of his childhood in poverty. A child raised by a never-married mother is more than 7 times more likely to be poor than a child raised in an intact marriage" [4].

· "A child living alone with a single mother is 14 times more likely to suffer serious physical abuse than is a child living with both biological parents united in marriage. A child whose mother cohabits with a man who is not the child's father is 33 times more likely to suffer serious physical abuse" [4].

Two parents for every child should be the desire of all for us, yet there are serious pros and cons to each side of the marriage question. Marriage is a serious step but teen marriages and young adult marriages can work. A couple seeking to be married can do well if they have the loving, practical, and prayerful support of their families.

Lori and Bob were 15 years old when Lori became pregnant. They both planned to attend college and didn't see how they could raise a child and go to school. They planned to get married as soon as they graduated from college. Lori spent part of her junior year of high school in a special school for pregnant girls away from home and lived in a maternity home. After the baby was born, Lori returned to high school for her senior year. After graduation, new mother Lori and baby went away for the summer. Lori took this time to think and pray about the future. She married Bob when she returned home. Years later, Lori and Bob attended their 10th high school reunion and their former classmates shared the changes in their lives. Many recounted divorces and multiple marriages. Because Bob and Lori, who married at 18, were still married, they gave the couple a standing ovation. We need to affirm marriage as God's plan for families, and marriage can be a positive answer to an unexpected pregnancy.

Notes:

[1] "Fertility, Family Planning, and Reproductive Health of U.S. Women: Data from the 2002 National Survey of Family Growth." Vital and Health Statistics, Series 23, Number 25, December 2005. U.S. Dept. of Health and Human Services, Centers for Disease Control and Prevention, National Center for Health Statistics.
[2] Daniel Lichter and Deborah Roempke Graefe, "Finding a Mate? The Marital and Cohabitation Histories of Unwed Mothers," in Lawrence Wu and Barbara Wolfe (eds.), Out of Wedlock: Trends, Causes and Consequences of Non-marital Fertility. New York: Russell Sage Foundation, 2001.
[3] Naomi Seiler. "Is Teen Marriage A Solution?" April 2002. Center for Law and Social Policy. www.clasp.org
[4] Patrick Fagan, Robert Rector, Kirk Johnson, and America Peterson. "The Positive Effects of Marriage: A Book of Charts." The Heritage Foundation. 2002.

[5] Timothy Grall. "Custodial Mothers and Fathers and Their Child Support: 2005." Issued August 2007 by the U.S. Census Bureau and the U.S. Department of Commerce Economics and Statistics Administration.

Prayer:
Lord Jesus, we thank You for the value and sanctity of human life. We pray that You will help us stand beside our daughter if she decides to marry, providing the practical and spiritual help that will aid her marriage in becoming a long-term success.

To Do:
Have your daughter and the young man each take a sheet of paper. Title it "What I'm looking for in a Husband/Wife." Tell them to list everything honestly. If she wants a 6'4" quarterback with blue eyes, she should write it down. They should be honest about any fantasies they have about a lifelong mate.

On another sheet, they should each write a list of what they feel that God wants for them in a marriage partner.

On a third sheet of paper, each should evaluate the other in terms of what God wants for a mate and what they want for a mate. Every desired characteristic that is not met should be examined to see if they are willing to give up that desire. They must choose to be content in marriage and rid themselves of unrealistic expectations. They must be willing to accept the other person as they are.

What are the struggles and blessings in your own marriage?

Share honestly with the young couple the struggles of your marriage and the blessings of your marriage.

Call Focus on the Family at 1-800-A-FAMILY (232-6459) and order the booklet "Five Reasons Why You Need the Piece of Paper" or the set titled "God's View of Cohabitation".

25. Teen Marriage Success

Marriage should be honored by all. Hebrews 13:4a (NIV)

Suggested Reading: Psalm 128   The Blessings of Home

The first three years of marriage appear to be quite critical, as the number of divorces jumps more drastically between the first and third years than it does from 3 years to 10 years [1]. While waiting to get married until after the age of 23 does reduce the number of dissolved marriages by the 10th anniversary to 20.2%, none of these numbers prove that teen marriages are doomed to certain failure.

Cumulative percent of first marriages still intact at interview time:

Age married	1 year since marriage	3 yrs	5 yrs	10yrs
Under 18	93.3%	76.4%	65.8%	51.9%
18-19 yrs	89.6%	79.9%	71.7%	60.8%
20-22 yrs	94.4%	85.0%	78.5%	68.1%
23+ yrs	96.5%	91.3%	86.7%	79.8%

In order to have a successful marriage, the young couple will need quite a bit of physical, emotional, and spiritual support. Discuss these issues with your daughter, your family, and the young man and his family when evaluating the potential for a successful marriage:

Is the young couple generally responsible and mature?

Have they done well in school?

Do they follow through on projects?

Do they love each other?

Is this a relationship that has a solid foundation?

Do they have the same spiritual background?

Will the church stand with them in this marriage?

Do they value the same things?

Are they willing to commit themselves to each other and their child?

Does the couple have the support of both their families?

Will the families provide encouragement and a sounding board to the couple?

Does the couple have any money saved?

Do they have any work experience?

Do they have any skills that will bring in money?

Will both families commit to providing practical help in the early years (e.g., caring for the baby while parents work, letting them live at home, loaning money, etc.)?

What boundaries can all three families establish so that relationships remain healthy and have room to grow and mature?

A study published in July 2002 reestablishes the fact that children do best when they live with married parents. The children are less likely to live in poverty, less likely to worry about food, and less likely to exhibit behavior problems. The parents are more likely to read to the child. This study called, "The Kids Are All Right? Children's Well Being And the Rise in Co-Habitation" was done by the Urban Institute Analysts Greg Acs and Sandi Nelson.

Preparation for marriage through marriage counseling is critical. The video series "A Biblical Portrait of Marriage," by Bruce Wilkerson of Walk Through The Bible [2], could be helpful.

Notes:

[1] "Fertility, Family Planning, and Reproductive Health of U.S. Women: Data from the 2002 National Survey of Family Growth." Vital and Health Statistics, Series 23, Number 25, December 2005. U.S. Dept. of Health and Human Services, Centers for Disease Control and Prevention, National Center for Health Statistics.

[2] A Biblical Portrait of Marriage video series and workbook. Walk Thru the Bible. www.walkthru.org

Prayer:

Creator God, we thank You that even scientists recognize the benefits of marriage. We thank You that the family is Your good idea. Help us all to work with this couple to build their marriage.

To Do:

What do you think the benefits of marriage include?

What do you see as the benefits to your grandchild?

How would your daughter's marriage to the father of her child be beneficial?

How would it be risky?

Is your own marriage strong?

If you are divorced, why did it happen?

Does your marriage experience color your thoughts of your daughter marrying?

Check out the studies by Ruddy and Rector that affirm the many benefits of marriage at www.heritage.org.

26. The Importance of a Father

As a father has compassion on his children, so the Lord has compassion on those who fear him. Psalm 103:13 (NIV)

Suggested Reading: Psalm 103   Papa God

At Assist PRC, we use the "Dads U." course to teach men about the attributes of a good father. According to this curriculum, a good father has Godly priorities, is a pacesetter, and is a partner to the mother of his children. He also protects and provides for them.

Priorities are the foundational in determining what we will do with our lives. Jesus desires us to have productive lives. We know that when fathers are involved in the lives of their children, the boys and girls will be more independent, self-reliant and more successful in school. We seek to point to the truth that if we make it a priority to follow and obey our Heavenly Father, His good plans lead us to success.

Pacesetter is another characteristic of a father. Dads help their children get started in life by guiding and disciplining the child with consistent loving attention. We are reminded to "endure hardship as discipline; God is treating you as sons. For what son is not disciplined by his father" Hebrews 12:7. A father must be around his children and know them well in order to provide direction and loving discipline.

A father should be a **Partner**. Mothers and fathers are to work together in cooperation to provide a loving, stable environment for their child. When a father figure is not available through the birth dad, grandfather, uncle or some other responsible male who promises to be involved throughout the lifetime of the child, this is a good time to consider an adoption plan so the child will have the benefit of both a mother (female) and father (male).

The father is a **Protector** and **Provider** who keeps women and children from harm. A father is to protect and provide financially, physically, emotionally and (most importantly) spiritually. He must be mature in all these areas if he is to give protection and provision.

Notes:
[1] "Dad's U Parenting Curriculum." Hope Pregnancy Center. www. hopepc.com

Prayer:
Abba Father, Thank you for your example of a loving Dad. Help me to encourage my daughter to really think about how she will provide a father for her child.

To Do:
In what ways was your father a good example? Can you write him a thank you letter or a poem of praise for Dads?

How have you tried to be a good parent? How did you succeed?

What does our culture say about the importance of fathers when we see 30% of children born to single moms?

Review Psalm 103 and note all the ways God is a good Father:
Priority

Pacesetter

Partner

Protector

Provider

Praise the Fatherhood of God in word, song, art, dance, etc.

27. Should She Parent Alone?

For God did not give us a spirit of timidity, but a spirit of power, of love and of self-discipline. 2 Timothy 1:7 (NIV)

Suggested Reading: 2 Timothy 1:3-7   Lois, Eunice and Timothy

The pregnancy resource center can educate your daughter about the realities (both the blessings and the difficulties) of parenting her child alone. It is important for both girls and boys to be involved with a father figure as they are growing up. If your daughter decides to parent her child, you and your husband need to decide if you will commit to being involved in the child's life. Single moms can do an outstanding job of parenting. My father died when I was nine and my mother raised three daughters alone. But single moms must be mature and well prepared if they are going to be successful parents.

If your daughter is under 18 years old, she will probably need to live with responsible adults. If you feel she cannot stay in your home, think of alternative housing solutions. Are there relatives who would let your daughter and her child live with them? Resist any efforts to let her live unmarried with her boyfriend, even if it is with his parents.

Some parents commit to having their daughter and her child live in the house with them. This can be difficult but it can also be wonderful. For centuries, multiple generations of family lived and worked together. Immigrant families of today often still do so. All family life can be stressful at times, but it can also be very helpful to all. It is important to have a signed set of rules in place before the child is born. This arrangement needs to provide for independence for the young mother and her child. It could be that they both live in her bedroom or they may have a larger space in the basement or other part of the house. It needs to be understood that your daughter is the mother of the child and all major responsibilities for the child must rest solely on her shoulders. Clearly state what role you are willing to take in the child's upbringing. Will you provide room and board for free or will you expect rent? Divide household chores and responsibilities. Discuss and sign a contract about what babysitting services you will provide.

If your daughter is 18 years or older and desires to live away from home, there may be a maternity home that will allow her and her child to live there while she attends college. Have your daughter look at the cost of apartments. She should check the housing board at church, if they have one, to see if there are women looking for roommates. Some couples looking for a nanny will allow her to bring her own child into the house and care for it along with the other children.

Take time to understand what your daughter is feeling. What are her dreams for the future?

What part will the father of the child play?

Will the father of the child willingly provide financial support?

Is he the type of person you want to be involved in your family for many years to come? Or should you ask him to legally relinquish his rights? This will release him from the obligation to support the child for 18 years.

A woman who is planning to be a single parent needs to have medical insurance. If she is a full-time student, she may be covered by the parent's insurance but very rarely will her baby be given any coverage. The state of Virginia makes available a low-cost insurance for children of single parents. Single parents must also have a will specifying who will care for the child if the parent should become disabled or die. The pregnancy resource center can help you discover the community resources that are available to answers these needs.

You only need to skim current newspapers to see that many grandparents are raising their grandchildren. The job of a single parent is very difficult for young mothers. Some will practically abandon their children into the care of their own parents. You need to evaluate the chances of this happening to your family.

A mature, responsible, determined, and well-planned single parent can be successful. Having a supportive family, church, and community will make the job easier. Many pregnancy resource centers have an on-going support group for single moms where the girls increase their skills and enjoy fellowship with other single moms and their children. Some Mothers of Preschoolers (MOPS) groups are also equipped to help single moms. These support groups can provide times of encouragement.

Prayer:
Dear Lord Who Provides (Jehovah Jireh), teach us to not be afraid of the future. Through the power of Your Holy Spirit, help us work with love and planning for the success of our daughter as a single parent. May we recognize You can provide all we need as we put our trust in You.

To Do:
With your daughter, create a time line of the next 10 years of her life. These dates can be flexible, but it is helpful for everyone to understand she needs to grow and mature so she is not still living with you when her own child is 18 years old.

Record here target dates for...
Completion of her education:

Completion of her job training:

The date she expects to have full-time employment:

Date the child will start school:

When she thinks she will have enough money for her own housing:

Create a plan of how she will provide babysitting or childcare while she is at work and school:

Below, or on a sheet of paper, help your daughter make a budget. Expenses that should be included for the mother and child are:
Tithe
Rent
Utilities
Food
Clothes
Education
Transportation
Entertainment
Child Care
Medical Care
Savings
See www.crown.org for many budgeting resources and ideas.

Make a contract with your daughter about the following topics. Some sample ideas are shown.

Her Privileges
• Use of TV (specify hours and/or shows, and where the TV will be located)
• Use of phone (specify hours; will she have her own line? Who will pay for the phone line and the usage charges? Talk about both the house phone and cell phones)
• Use of car (specify gas/mileage reimbursement. Who will pay for her insurance?)
• Use of a computer and the Internet.
• Visitors to the house (specify who will be allowed to visit, what hours visitors are allowed, and what rooms they are allowed to visit in.)

Her Responsibilities for her health
• Attend doctor appointments.
• Follow doctor's orders and recommendations (diet, exercise, medicine, etc.).
• Attend childbirth preparation classes.
• Attend counseling appointments.
• Abstaining from sexual activity.
• Abstaining from smoking, drugs, and alcohol.
• Be in bed at a specific time each night.

• Be out of bed at a specific time each morning and dressed for the day.
• Who will pay for doctor visits, medicine, and insurance premiums?
• What transportation will she need to attend doctor appointments?

Her Responsibilities in the house
• Keep her room clean and orderly (bed made up, floor vacuumed, furniture dusted, waste baskets emptied, bed sheets changed).
• Help set and clear the dining table.
• Help with grocery shopping.
• Put dirty dishes in dishwasher (or wash them) immediately after a meal.
• Clean up counters, stovetop, and refrigerator.
• Wash, dry, fold, and put away her laundry promptly.
• Keep her bathroom clean (sinks and shower clean, floor swept, mirror clean, toilet clean, trash can empty).
• Participate in meal preparation; Cook alone.

Her Responsibilities at school
• Attend school regularly.
• Complete homework before watching TV.
• Who will babysit the baby while she's at school? Who will pay for this?
• What grades are expected of her?

Her Responsibilities at work
• Attend her job promptly as scheduled, and work a full shift.
• Call work if an emergency prevents her attendance.
• What transportation will she need to work?
• Who will babysit the baby while she's at work? Who will pay for this?
• What expecations do you have about how she will use the money earned from a job?

Her Spiritual Responsibilities
• Attend church at least weekly.
• Make progress on a personal Bible study book.

Her Preparation for the Future
• Adoption counseling and planning?
• Pre-marital counseling and planning?
• Birth plan and childbirth education.
• Education on parenting skills, relationship skills, and childcare skills.

Decide on consequences for failure to meet any of the rules you set out. Be sure to stress the importance of those rules (if any) that will result in expulsion from the home if broken (e.g. doing drugs, sex, etc.).

Both you and your daughter should begin reading educational books such as:

"Boundaries" by Dr. Henry Cloud and John Townsend. Zondervan. 2002.

"Successful Single Parenting" by Gary Richmond. Harvest House Publishers. 1998.

"Tony Evans Speaks Out on Single Parenting" by Tony Evans. Moody Publishers. 2000.

28. Should We Adopt the Baby?

These are the things you are to do: Speak the truth to each other, and render true and sound judgment in your courts. Zechariah 8:16 (NIV)

Suggested Reading: John 14:1-17   Jesus Is The Truth

When faced with the prospect of a teenage daughter's pregnancy, many parents can't face any of the options. They are morally opposed to abortion. They fear their daughter parenting will ruin her life yet they hestitate to imagine their grandchild being raised by a family through adoption. Even the prospect of an open adoption, where the mother can remain in contact with her child to various degrees, does not satisfy some grandparents. Finances are another reason to contemplate the adoption of your grandchild: there are tax benefits for having dependants and if you adopt the baby he or she can be placed on your health insurance. In these situations, many grandparents consider adopting the child themselves. According to the U.S. Census Bureau, in 2004 over 2.4 million grandparents were primary caregivers for their grandchildren, though this is not always via adoption.

In years past, when women had children well into their forties, sometimes a mother would pass her daughter's child off as her own. Recently I was talking to a friend and helping her with her genealogy. We came to the name of a person who had been raised by grandparents as the sibling of her birth mother. Even though all of the principal persons were dead, this situation was still a huge family "secret." The "secret" was widely known and often discussed in whispers by the family and their friends. I am entirely opposed to grandparents adopting their grandchild if they plan to pretend it is their own child and perpetuate a family secret. I have never found that family secrets bring good but have often found they bring distrust, anger, and lie upon lie. Secrecy causes shame, guilt, fear, isolation and defensiveness. But honesty promotes trust, peace, acceptance, and contentment.

If you plan to formally adopt your grandchild, the truth should be spoken from the beginning. The child's mother should be identified as such. Because adoption is not possible without both birth parents relinquishing their rights, the adoption should not be informal but needs to be done legally with a lawyer. If you decide to parent your grandchild as the "legal guardian" or custodian, you will likewise need the legal paperwork to prove that you have legal rights concerning the child.

As with every decision about a woman's pregnancy, the decision to make an adoption plan, either in the family or outside of it, must be the mother's well-thought out and fully supported choice. She must recognize that by placing her child with her own parents or another family member she has forever forfeited her role as mother to the child. One of the main complications with adoptions inside the family is that, when a daughter matures and is on her feet, she often feels she has the right to reclaim her child. There is no need for me to explain the anguish and turmoil this causes to all involved.

To prevent any hidden agendas, if an adoption is made inside the family, the legal papers should contract between the daughter and the adopting parents outlining the expectations and promises. Some parents specify in the contract the conditions under which they would return the child to their daughter (i.e., when she finished college, or gets married, etc.).

All of these arrangements need to be thought out before the adoption is final because they will influence the way the child is raised and what the child is told. Adoption within a family brings a unique set of problems that need to be carefully thought out with sound advice from your lawyer, your pastor, and a council of family members.

Prayer:
Heavenly Father, we are grateful for Your good idea of creating families to help each other. We thank You for our family, our daughter, and this expected grandchild. We cling to the promise that if we ask You for wisdom You will give it.

To Do:

What would cause you to adopt your grandchild?

Why would you not consider adopting your grandchild?

What are some secrets in your family?

What impact have those secrets had on the family?

If considering adoption, ask your pastor or a PRC for a list of supportive adoption lawyers or agencies in your area.

29. Should She Make An Adoption Plan?

If any of you lacks wisdom, he should ask God, who gives generously to all without finding fault and it will be given to him. James 1:5 (NIV)

Suggested Reading: James 1:2-8   True Faith

Presently, less than three percent of birthmothers in America will choose adoption for their child. Unfortunately our culture considers adoption to be more horrific than abortion! God has always affirmed adoption - after all, we are adopted into God's family ourselves!

Today's adoption plan has many options including the confidential adoption of past generations. There is also open adoption, in which the birth mother has visitation rights and can communicate with her child as he or she grows. Even in closed adoption, most agencies can facilitate the routing of photos and letters between the adoptive parents and the birth mother even though there is no visitation. When these options are explained through adoption education to the birth mother, it can help her realize she can know something about her child throughout life. This can help her make the mature, selfless, and difficult choice of adoption.

It is important for the pregnant woman to understand all of the options open to her. Your local pregnancy resource center, Bethany Christian Services, or other licensed adoption agencies can educate your daughter to the positive realities of adoption. At Assist Pregnancy Center, we examine the realities of abortion, parenting, and adoption with each young woman we counsel.

Note that the father of the baby must relinquish his parental rights before an adoption can take place. If he refuses to relinquish his rights, the mother is forced into parenting or must go to court to attempt to get his rights terminated involuntarily. In some situations, failure to respond to published notification of pending adoption can result in de facto termination of the father's rights. Consult with an adoption agency or adoption lawyer in your area for more details.

What are some reasons that a baby should be placed for adoption? I think the most important consideration is the answer to the question, "Will the birth mother be able to provide a dependable, mature father figure throughout the child's life?" Will her father, uncle, brother, or other family member vow to be actively involved with the child in every stage of its development? If not, adoption should be considered.

Is the young woman an immature person herself? Has she had poor success in following through with her responsibilities? Does she lack job skills and aptitude? If so, adoption should be considered.

Is the baby seen as a way to hold on to a boyfriend? Is the baby looked at as a provider of unconditional love for the young mother? Is the baby seen as a trophy that can be displayed to friends? If so, adoption should be considered.

Is the birth mother involved in a sexually promiscuous lifestyle? Does she use drugs or alcohol? Does she abuse her body in other ways? If so, adoption should be considered.

Does she lack family support and the backing of a strong, committed community? If so, adoption should be considered.

Don't press a young woman to place for adoption simply because there are tens of thousands of couples wishing for a child. She must see adoption as the best solution for her and for her child's future well being.

I remember many years ago a 14 year old client who came in multiple times for a pregnancy test, hoping to find herself pregnant. She lived in a household comprised of several generations of females and their offspring, all dependant on welfare for survival. She voiced to me repeatedly that if she could get pregnant, the government would give her an apartment of her own, a salary, and medical benefits. Even though I assured her this was not the case for a 14 year old, she continued her lifestyle until she did indeed get pregnant. She found, to her sorrow, her assumptions about an easy life provided by the state were a myth. Most states require single mothers to work to receive any help. Often low-income housing and other benefits are only provided for a limited time. The condition and location of public housing is frequently quite poor.

Even before Hurricane Katrina displaced tens of thousands of people, most cities nationwide already lacked the resources to offer subsidized housing to those living in the area. The largest cities have tens of thousands on waiting lists for public housing assistance, including more than 30,000 in Washington, D.C., 250,000 in New York City, and 85,000 in Los Angeles [1].

It is important to have each pregnant teen understand what is required in parenting for 18 years. Adoption can provide a stable, loving home with a mother and father for the child. Adoption can free a young woman to follow her dreams.

At Assist Pregnancy Center we encourage each client to look at adoption. I have never had a mother express disappointment that she placed the child for adoption. But many clients who are single moms or who had abortions have come back to tell us that they wish they had made other choices.

Notes:
[1] - "Katrina Victims Unwelcome in Some Towns, " by Juliana Barbassa, Associated Press Writer. October 4, 2004.

Prayer:
Dear Father, help us to listen to our daughter and her desires for her future. Enable us to help her weigh the pros and cons of making an adoption plan for her baby. Thank You for adopting us into Your family.

To Do:
Ask your PRC, Bethany Christian Services, or another adoption agency about adoption education for your daughter.

Ask your PRC to give you a list of maternity homes where adoption will be discussed while your daughter resides there.

Have your daughter journal:
"Why adoption would be a good choice for me…"
"Why adoption would not be a good choice for me…"
"Why adoption would be a good choice for my baby…"
"Why adoption would not be a good choice for my baby..."

Why adoption would or would not be a good choice for your daughter:

Why adoption would or would not be a good choice for your daughter's child:

Discuss with your daughter your journaled thoughts on adoption and compare them to hers.

Name friends who are adopted:

Name friends who have adopted:

Do some research on the Internet and makes lists of famous people were adopted themselves, famous people who have made an adoption plan for their child, and famous people have adopted children into their family:

30. Our Hope For The Next Five Years

When I was a child, I talked like a child, I thought like a child, I reasoned like a child. When I became a man, I put childish ways behind me. 1 Corinthians 13:11 (NIV)

Suggested Reading: Proverbs 16   Godly Wisdom

Five years from now, the expected child will be almost ready for kindergarten. The child will have progressed from a newborn infant to toddler to young child. With each passing year his skills and world will blossom with new potential.

In five years your daughter will likely have left her teenage years behind. She may have graduated from college, and will most likely have a great deal more work experience. If she has placed the child for adoption or is married, the crisis pregnancy pain may have largely faded from her emotions. The experience of pregnancy and bearing a child will likely have matured her and given her a desire for a solid foundation for her future.

Help your daughter examine the next five years of her life:

Write on a piece of paper your daughter's birthday for the next five years. Have your daughter dream about and record what she would like each of those years to mean for her physically, mentally, emotionally, and spiritually. Also list the people who may be involved in these dreams (the father of the baby, the child, etc.).

On a second sheet of paper tape a snapshot of your daughter from each of the previous five years. Beside each photo, write comments about how she grew physically, mentally, emotionally, and spiritually during that year. If she only grew in a few areas, note reasons for her lack of growth. Share with her the observations you recorded.

On a third piece of paper, write about your own life (corresponding to her current age and for the next five years). Use photos to illustrate the years of your life. Beside each of your pictures, list each year's high and low points physically, mentally, emotionally, and spiritually. Be honest with your daughter about any mistakes you made in your dating, your lifestyle, or your habits.

I hope both you and your daughter are journaling your experiences during the pregnancy. If the child is placed for adoption, copies from selected pages of either journal can be a touching gift to the adoptive parents. If your daughter parents the child, the journal could be a nice memento to give the child when he is older.

Prayer:
Papa God, we pray that everyone involved in waiting for the birth of this child will grow and mature. Help us to identify and put away our childish behavior.

To Do:
Do the suggested activity pages described (above) in this chapter.

Encourage your daughter to also do the suggested activity pages.

Sit at a table with your daughter and share honestly about your life.

Write out the five sayings in Proverbs 16 that spoke to you most:

Why did they speak to you?

31. Childcare Responsibilities

I am the good shepherd; I know my sheep and my sheep know me – just as the Father knows me and I know the Father – and I lay down my life for the sheep. John 10:14 (NIV)

Suggested Reading: John 10:1-18   The Good Shepherd

Some of the hard lessons that a first-time mother of any age learns are:
· Babies take a lot of care.
· Parenting is a 24 hour/day, 7 day/week job.
· Babies cry. Many times you can't figure out why the baby is crying. You may be up all night wondering if the baby is sick or just demanding.
· Babies and mothers get sick. Who will care for them?
· Babies are expensive. The medical bills alone can tax the resources of a single parent.
· Parenting can be boring when you are home alone with the baby. When friends want you to go out with them, it can be difficult to find someone you trust to take care of your child.
· If a young mother is working, who will provide daycare?

There are three categires of child care: family care, home daycare (whether at someone else's home, or at your home with a nanny), and day care center. In 2001, 56% of children aged three to five (not yet enrolled in kindergarten) were enrolled in a day care center. About 23% of children received care from family, and 14% attended a home day care (non-relatives) [1]. Family care is when a biological relative of the child provides care while the child's mother is away at work or school. Home daycare is when a non-relative cares for your child, either at your home or at their own home.

One advantage of family care is that you may be more confident that your relatives will look out for the best interests of the child and will teach your child values that you hold in common. Family care works best when the family has good relationships, flexible schedules, and ability and willingness to help. Even so, be prepared to make a formal business-like arrangment that specifies the expectations from each party (about feeding, discipline, sleep, crying, play time and authority), and including any payment schedule. You should also develop a backup plan to handle times when your relative is ill or travels.

When choosing a home daycare provider, first learn about your state's licensing requirements so that you can observe whether the rules are being followed and so that you can ask good interview questions. You should make a backup plan for days when the home daycare provider is traveling or ill. According to the National Association for the Education of Young Children (NAEYC, www.naeyc.org), home daycare providers should not take more than two babies under 30 months, five kids under five, and two additional school-aged children unless they have an assistant. Ask to see a schedule of daily activities, the house rules, emergency exit plan, and the discipline philosophies of the provider. You can also check with your state's social service department to see if any complaints have been lodged against the provider. Home daycare may provide the opportunity to play with a mixed group of ages, and may be less expensive than a daycare center.

Most daycare centers have few openings for infants because they require so much hands-on care. Because of waiting lists, you may have to sign up for infant daycare more than six months in advance! It is important to arrange for daycare before the child is born. You should know the policies of the childcare facility; many will not accept a child under 8 weeks old. Daycare centers are regulated, so they may offer a more structured setting than other care options. Look for a center that has the smallest number of children per adult that you can afford. The NAEYC recommends that daycare centers have one caregiver for every three babies if there are six infants in a group, and one caregiver for every four babies if there are eight babies in a group. Eight babies should be the maximum number in any group. In addition, there should be one caregiver for three children in a group of six, a 1:4 ratio for eight children in a group, 1:5 ratio for ten children in a group, and 1:4 ratio for 12 children in a group (the maximum group size).

Observe several hours at a daycare center to see how the caregivers interact with children, group size, and equipment available. Most daycare centers have relatively strict rules about drop-off and pick-up times, among other rules, so be sure to get all of the rules in writing and read them carefully. Make a backup plan for days when your child is sick and you are not permitted to take him to the daycare center. A young mother should investigate the cost of daycare while deciding whether to parent or place for adoption.

In looking for a daycare center, be sure to choose one:
· Licensed by the county or state.
· That has trained personnel.
· With a small number of children for each adult.
· Televisions are not used to entertain the children.
· There are many supervised opportunities for physical activity.
· One that is clean, bright, safe and with a well-planned schedule.
· And one where Jesus is honored.

Visit the facility as a drop-in, if possible. By showing up without an appointment, you are more likely to see the true manner of operations. A young mother should spend several hours (on different days of the week) quietly observing at a daycare facility to evaluate the quality of care she can expect for her child.

Check your church's bulletin board for childcare resources. There may be other young mothers who offer childcare. Some churches offer preschool or daycare. A few companies and some schools have daycare facilities on their grounds.

Finding daycare for your baby is time consuming but very important. Accomplish this task before the baby is born.

Notes:
[1] - U.S. Department of Education, National Center for Education Statistics. 2006. Digest of Education Statistics, 2005 (NCES 2006-030), Table 42.

Prayer:
Lord, my Shepherd (Jehovah Raah), we thank You for tenderly caring for

us as a shepherd cares for his lambs. Help us to find qualified and loving daycare for our grandchild. We rely on Your protection and recognize You are all we need in this challenge.

To Do:
Write about the following:
How is Jesus a Good Shepherd?

What is the difference between the Good Shepherd and the thief?

How is the Good Shepherd like a good parent?

List good child care options in your area. Ask your friends for recommendations.

Have your daughter practice with you how to interview a childcare provider.

If you haven't done so already, make a contract with your daughter for the childcare you will provide (when the child is sick and can't attend daycare, while she is at school, when she is at church activities with no child care, etc.). How many hours each week will you provide care? How much advance notice do you require?

Help your daughter determine what other care the child will need if she is parenting. Make notes of that conversation here.

What is the expected weekly income your daughter will have after giving birth?

From your research, how much will childcare cost each week?

Will her expected income cover the costs of daycare?

If not, what options exist?

What impact does this discussion have on your decision about parenting versus adoption?

32. The Baby is Born

For You created my inmost being; You knit me together in my mother's womb. I praise You because I am fearfully and wonderfully made; Your works are wonderful, I know that full well. Psalm 139:13 – 14 (NIV)

Suggested Reading: Psalm 139:13 – 18   Wonderfully Made

In preparing for the birth of the baby the experience gained from many sources will come into play. Your OB/GYN will have discussed pain management, labor, and delivery choices with your daughter. In most areas today, it's possible to have your child in a hospital, birthing center, or at home. Usually the birthing center or hospital setting is chosen for the delivery of a first child. You may offer to go with your daughter as she tours the facility, offer to be her birth coach, and offer to attend the appropriate classes to prepare you for this opportunity. If you are not available, who will be her birth partner?

The doctor, the pregnancy resource center, or an adoption agency will have counseled your daughter regarding parenting or placing her child. It is beneficial to have your daughter write out a birth plan, regardless of the option she has chosen. This birth plan should include all the reasons why adoption or parenting was deemed the best choice for your daughter and for the child. Your doctor may be able to provide a birth plan template or many samples are available on the Internet (try www.birthplan.com or search for "birth plan template" in a search engine).

If your daughter has chosen to parent, the birth plan should also include:

· Whether she's going to breastfeed or bottle feed her child.

· Who will be allowed to visit and when.

· What photos or videos will be taken during and after birth .

· Whether the baby will be housed in the nursery or the your daughter's room.

· Whether a baby boy will be circumcised and, if he will, when.

· Any preferences she has for her own medical care during her stay.

If your daughter is making an adoption plan, her birth plan should include:

· Who will be allowed to visit and when.

· How often she wants her adoption counselor to visit.

· What photos or videos will be taken during and after birth.

· Where the baby will be housed during its hospital stay.

· What level of interaction she would like to have with the baby.

· What level of interaction the adoptive parents can have at the hospital.

· Whether she will have a dedication service and, if so, when and what format the service will take.

· And any preferences she has for her own medical care during her hospital stay.

Regardless of whether or not your daughter will be parenting the baby, she will need to spend time preparing for birth. This may include watching videos, reading books about labor and delivery, and attending childbirth classes. There are a number of different childbirth methods available today. Your daughter should spend some time researching each of them and determining which sounds like something that will work for her. Once she has made this decision, she should find and enroll in classes. Be sure to do this before the third trimester begins – some methods require 16 weeks of classes. Classes offered at the hospital tend to fill quickly. Keep in mind that a due date is just an estimate, so she should be finished with her classes at least two weeks prior to her due date to allow for an early delivery.

Prayer:

Creator God (Elohim), we thank You for our daughter and her child. We pray that You will guide the doctors. Please help our daughter have a safe, speedy, and uncomplicated delivery.

To Do:

Find out about any rules for guests in the labor and delivery department.

Have your daughter make a list of the people she wants at the hospital while she's giving birth. Separate the list into those who are allowed in the delivery room and those who are to remain in the waiting room. Have her notify these people of her preferences. Record these people here:

Delivery Room   Waiting Room

Decide whether the father of the baby and/or his family will be present and what their involvement in the birth will be. Record your plans:

If your daughter is making an adoption plan, she will need to decide if she desires to have the adoptive parents present for the birth experience or if they will be notified after delivery. Record your plans:

Verify that any legal issues have been taken care of by the agency or lawyer assisting with the adoption.

Help your daughter investigate the different childbirth methods and locate classes for her selected choice. Record her choice and plans for childbirth education:

Share your positive birthing experiences with your daughter to help alleviate her fear. Discuss the differences in the birth experience today (based on your research) with the experience when you last had a child.

Take some time to remember your first birth experience and journal about your fears and anxieties. Tell whether they were unfounded or how you got through them during the experience. Share your entry with your daughter.

My fears and anxieties about giving birth the first time were:

My fears and anxieties were different from reality in these ways:

My childbirth experience(s) were...

Make arrangements to have flowers, balloons or a plant delivered to your daughter after childbirth.

Discuss with your daughter the practice of videotaping births. Investigate the hospital or birthing center policy on taping a birth. Listen carefully to her preferences and write down what aspects of the delivery she's comfortable having taped, if any:

33. Dedication Service

And the child grew and became strong; He was filled with wisdom, and the grace of God was upon Him. Luke 2:40 (NIV)

Suggested Reading: Luke 2:21 – 40   Jesus Dedicated

After the birth of a baby, the Scriptures give several examples of children being taken to the temple for dedication. Jesus and Samuel are two examples of this practice. If your daughter is placing the child for adoption, it can be important to have a private ceremony dedicating the child to the Lord.   The service can be held at the hospital in your daughter's room or in the hospital chapel. Very close friends and family, a pastor, and the adoptive couple can be included.   This will be a time to bless your daughter and her child.

The purpose of the dedication service is:

· To recognize the unique value of the child's life.

· To thank God for your daughter's courage and selflessness in placing her child with a loving mother and father.

· To pray God's blessing on the adoptive couple as they parent the child.

· It is a formal time for your daughter to relinquish her child into the care its new parents.

· It is a time to bless your daughter, the child, and the adoptive parents.

Songs that could be used during the service include:
>Jesus Loves Me;
>Blessed the Tie that Binds
>Take My Life and Let It Be
>God Will Take Care of You
>They That Wait Upon the Lord

Through it All
Near to the Heart of God
What a Friend We Have in Jesus

The pastor could give a short devotional covering the idea that each of us is adopted into God's family using a story from the Bible. Some to choose from include:

Moses and Pharaoh's daughter
Samuel and Eli
Esther and Mordecai
Abraham and Eliazar
Joseph accepting Jesus as his child

There might be time for the adopting couple to express their gratitude for the gift of their child. Your daughter could say a few words about why she felt the Lord led her to an adoption decision. The pastor could close with a prayer asking the Lord to comfort your daughter and your family, protect and guide the baby, and bless the new parents as they raise the child to know about the love of Jesus. The pastor can place his right hand on the child and say, "The Lord bless and keep you; the Lord make His face shine upon you and be gracious to you: the Lord turn His face toward you and give you peace." (Numbers 6:24-26, NIV) Your daughter can then hand the child to its new parents and everyone can spend a few minutes talking before leaving for their respective homes.

When your daughter arrives home, her bedroom should be clean and inviting with fresh flowers and a new teddy bear or stuffed animal to cuddle when she sleeps. Check with your daughter to see if she wants to be alone or if she would like company. It would be nice to have on hand some of her favorite foods for a welcome home meal and a video or other activity that she can enjoy with the entire family. She should receive post-adoption counseling from the adoption agency or lawyer. The counselor should be available to talk to her whenever she needs someone to hear how she is feeling.

If your daughter is parenting her child alone, be sure to be sensitive to her feelings with respect to a dedication service. Often a single mom will not wish to participate in a dedication service in front of the church with couples and their babies. It would be appropriate to arrange for her to participate in a private dedication service either at home or in a small chapel. Invite family and close friends who are pledging to be a support to your daughter as she parents this child.

The purpose of this service is:

·To rejoice in the birth of her child.

· To pray for your daughter as she finds others who will help her raise her child or as she undertakes this task on her own.

· To pray God's blessing on your daughter and her child.

· And affirm those who are covenanting with her to provide Godly examples (both male and female) for her child.

The pastor could give a brief devotional on a parent's privilege to lead a child to Christ and provide for the child physically, mentally, emotionally, and spiritually. The pastor should include not only your daughter in this challenge of a parent's responsibility, but also the male relative who is covenanting with your daughter to provide a consistent male role model to the child in lieu of a father. Songs that could be sung as part of this service are the same as previously listed. The pastor should close in prayer asking the Lord's blessing on the child and your daughter using Numbers 6:24 – 26.

Prayer:
Gracious Heavenly Father, we thank You for our daughter and her child. We pray that You will bless and lead them in the coming days.

To Do:
Talk with your daughter about having a dedication service. Discuss who should be invited, where you would like to hold it, what pastor can lead it, and the order of service. Spend some time together making a bulletin to give to the participants as a keepsake of the event. Write your plans here.

Who to invite:

Date, time, and location of dedication service:

Who will lead the service:

Order of Service:

34. Single Moms and Church

Let's see how inventive we can be in encouraging love and helping out, not avoiding worshiping together as some do but spurring each other on especially as we see the big day approaching. Hebrews 10:24-25 (MES)

Suggested Reading: Hebrews 10:19-25   Fellowship

A July 2002 report [1] on research conducted by the University of Pennsylvania's Center for Research on Religion and Urban Civil Society examined fragile families and child well-being. The research discovered that religious attendance was as important as socio-economic factors, such as income, in predicting the marriage of single mothers.

W. Bradford Wilcox, Assistant Professor of Sociology at the University of Virginia and author of this report, revealed that unwed mothers "are 90% more likely to marry within a year of that birth if they attend church" several times a month or more, compared with mothers who rarely attend. The report also showed that women who have given birth out-of-marriage tend to receive moral support rather than scorn from church.

Reverend Cedric Brown is quoted in the study, "In terms of unwed mothers, we don't coerce them to get married," but instead help them make decisions and encourage the father to take responsibility for the child. In his experience, he found that many of the unmarried men and women with children are young and need multiple kinds of support and guidance, which the church can provide.

I thought this was encouraging information for the parents of a single mom. I think it is good for daughters to recognize that church is likely to be a safe place for them to be. This study can give hope for the future, recognizing a secondary benefit of going to church is support from the congregation and an increased likelihood of marriage.

Attending church is also connected to better health for your daughter. The National Center on Addiction and Substance Abuse (CASA) at Columbia University has an annual back-to-school survey of attitudes on subtance abuse. The 2007 survey results showed that "teens who never attend religious services in a typical month have substance abuse risk scores that are almost double those of teens who attend weekly religious services" [2].

Prayer:

Dear Father, we are thankful that when we obey Your directives, such as joining together for worship, that we can find ourselves blessed in many ways.

Notes:

[1] "Then Comes Marriage: Religion, Race, and Marriage in Urban America." Dr. W. Bradford Wilcox. The Center for Research on Religion and Urban Civil Society, University of Pennsylvania. 2002.
[2] "National Survey of American Attitudes on Substance Abuse XII: Teens and Parents." August 2007. The National Center on Addiction and Substance Abuse at Columbia University. www.casacolumbia.org

To Do:

Write out the promises that God gives us in Hebrews 10:19-25:

List the actions that God desires from us:

Ask your Pastor about the ways your church brings encouragement and hope to single parents. If your church does not have a program for single parents, call other congregations in your area and check to see what they offer.

Appendix A:
Parental Authority
Over a Minor

Often parents have expressed their frustration in dealing with a teenager who is pregnant and being influenced by an older male. A parent does have some legal options when dealing with this situation.

NOTE: The educational information in this entire Appendix is NOT to be considered legal advice. For legal advice always consult a professional lawyer who is qualified to practice law in your locality. The author and Chalfont House shall have neither liability nor responsibility to any person or entity with respect to any loss or damage caused, or alleged to have been caused, directly or indirectly, by the information contained in this book.

1.   Confrontation with the Offending Party

It has been suggested that one approach to take before looking for legal redress is to meet with the man one-on-one in the presence of at least one (non-family) witness to discuss your concerns. The parents should question him to see if there is any authority figure in his life that he respects to underline how important authority is in all of our lives. If this elicits a response that he has no authority in his life, it is suggested that you discuss your investment in your child's life and your desire to see your child have a successful life and enter adulthood on a firm foundation. Ask him "What can we do to keep her focused on her best interests?" (i.e., finishing school, getting job skills, taking good physical care of herself and her child, continuing her education in college, etc.).

2.   The Doctrine of Parental Authority.

The government affirms that parents have authority over their minor children. The government also affirms that parents have the right and responsibility to bring up children in accordance with the parents' beliefs and expectations of behavior. The decision in *Williams v. Williams,* 24 Va. App. 778 (1997) reaffirmed that parents can protect their minor children

173

from outside influences that seek to undermine parental and family values. *Williams* confirms that parents have a fundamental/constitutional right to raise their children as they see fit, including preventing them from visiting others (including their grandparents) and that right may be abridged only upon a showing that denying another visitation rights with the child would cause actual harm to the child's health or welfare. Thus, a parent can forbid an individual who is interfering with the moral upbringing and child rearing of the family from having any contact with a minor.

3.   A CHINS (Child in Need of Services) Petition

A parent may petition the Court to have the child put under court supervision and authority. This often takes many months to accomplish. This would bring the full complement of the law, including police enforcement, detention, and health and human services into the lives of the family. The knowledge that this action is possible may help a rebellious teenager recognize that submitting to parental authority would be far less invasive than being under the authority of the juvenile justice system.

4.   Contributing to the Delinquency of a Minor

A criminal charge can be brought against a person who introduces a minor to improper behavior or provides the means for a minor to engage in improper behavior. This generally is enforced with respect to underage drinking or with use of illegal drugs. It is not usually effective with respect to sexual activity.

5.   Anti-trespass

A parent who is the deed holder (owner of the property) or lease holder (one who rents and enjoys the quiet possession of the leasehold (rented) property) may send a "No trespass" letter by certified mail return receipt requested to the individual who is influencing his/her minor child. If the individual comes onto the property after receipt of that letter, he/she can be arrested for trespass.

6.   Restraining Order

Where there has been some form of abuse or neglect of a child, the parent may seek a restraining order for immediate help. The restraining order forbids the individual from contacting the minor or coming onto the property. If he/she violates the restraining order, he/she can be arrested.

Appendix B:
Parental Rights
Regarding Abortion

NOTE: This educational information was correct, to the best of our knowledge, as of November 2007. NARAL (a pro-abortion agency) keeps close track of state laws that restrict access to abortion, and the information in this appendix is derived from their "State Profiles" which can be found at http://www.prochoiceamerica.org/choice-action-center/in_your_state/who-decides/. Note that the information at that website is couched in strong anti-life terms.

NOTE: This information is NOT to be considered legal advice. For legal advice, always consult a professional lawyer who is qualified to practice law in your locality. The author and Chalfont House shall have neither liability nor responsibility to any person or entity with respect to any loss or damage caused, or alleged to have been caused, directly or indirectly, by the information contained in this book.

Alabama law says that one parent must consent to the abortion in writing for an unemancipated minor under the age of 18. Consent can be circumvented in several ways.

Alaska law says one parent must consent to the abortion in writing for an unemancipated minor under the age of 17. A minor can circumvent consent by obtaining a court order. However, the law is currently not in effect because it was ruled unconstitutional (this ruling is under appeal). The result is that currently a parent is not notified nor can a parent stop the abortion.

Arizona law says one parent must consent to the abortion in writing for an unemancipated minor under the age of 18. A minor can circumvent this by obtaining a court order.

Arkansas law says one parent must consent to the abortion in writing for an unemancipated minor under the age of 18. A minor can circumvent this by obtaining a court order.

California law requires one parent to consent in writing. Consent can be circumvented by obtaining a court order. However, this law is not in effect because it has been ruled unconstitutional. The result is that currently a parent is not notified nor can a parent stop the abortion.

Colorado law requires an unemancipated minor under 18 to wait for an abortion until 48 hours after written notice has been delivered to one or both parents. Notification can be circumvented in several ways.

Connecticut law says that an unemancipated minor under 16 merely has to be counseled by a physician, nurse, physician's assistant, clergy member, or qualified counselor. Parents are not notified and are not required to give consent.

Delaware law says that one parent must be notified at least 24 hours in advance of an abortion on an unemancipated minor under 16. The waiting period allows the parents some time to discuss the matter with the minor before the abortion is performed. It does not allow the parents to prevent the abortion. Notification can be circumvented in several ways.

The District of Columbia (Washington DC) has no laws related to a minor's access to abortion.

Florida law requires a minor under the age of 18 to wait for an abortion until 48 hours after notice has been delivered to one parent. Notification can be circumvented in several ways.

Georgia law requires an unemacipated minor under 18 to wait 24 hours after notifying one parent. Notification can be waived under several circumstances. The waiting period allows the parents some time to discuss the matter with the minor before the abortion is performed. It does not allow the parents to prevent the abortion.

Hawaii has no laws related to a minor's access to abortion.

Idaho requires written consent of one parent before an unemancipated minor under 18 may have an abortion. Consent can be waived under several circumstances.

Illinois requires an unmarried or unemancipated minor under 18 to wait at least 48 hours after notification in person or by telephone to one parent, grandparent, or step-parent living in the house. Notification can be waived under several circumstances. However, this law in not being enforced because a court has issued a permanent injunction. The result is that currently a parent is not notified nor can a parent stop the abortion.

Indiana requires the written consent of one parent for an abortion to be performed on an unemancipated minor under 18. Consent can be circumvented by a court order.

Iowa requires an unmarried or unemancipated minor under 18 to wait at least 48 hours after notification in person or by certified mail to one parent, or a grandparent. Notification can be waived under several circumstances.

Kansas requires an unmarried or unemancipated minor under 18 to give notice to one parent; the minor must receive counsel while accompanied by a parent or interested adult over 21 who is not affiliated with the abortion provider. Notification can be waived under several circumstances.

Kentucky requires an unemancipated minor under 18 to have written consent of one parent.Consent can be waived by a court order.

Louisiana requires an unemancipated minor under 18 to have notorized written consent of one parent. Consent can be waived by a court order.

Maine requires that an unemancipated minor under 18 receive counsel and have written consent by one parent or adult family member. Consent can be waived by a court order or if the abortionist determines that the minor is mature enough to provide her own consent.

Maryland requires an unmarried minor under 18 who lives with a parent to notify the parent. The abortionist can waive the notification if he feels that parental notice would lead to physical or emotional abuse of the minor, or the minor is mature and capable of giving her own consent, or if notice would not be in the "best interest" of the minor.

Massachussets requires an unmarried minor under 18 to have written consent of one parent. Consent can be waived by a court order.

Michigan requires an unemancipated minor under 18 to have written consent of one parent. Consent can be waived by a court order.

Minnesota requires an unemancipated minor under 18 to wait at least 48 hours after written notification has been delivered to both parents. Notification can be waived by a court order.

Mississippi requires an unemancipated minor under 18 to have the written consent of one or both parents. Consent can be waived by a court order.

Missouri requires an unemancipated minor under 18 to have written consent of one parent.Consent can be waived by a court order.

Montana requires an unemancipated minor under 18 to wait at least 48 hours after a physician notifies one parent. A state court has placed an injunction against this law. The result is that currently a parent is not notified and cannot prevent the abortion.

Nebraska requires an unemancipated minor under 18 to wait at least 48 hours after written notice has been delivered to one parent. Notification can be waived by a court order.

Nevada requires an unmarried or unemancipated minor under 18 to notify one parent. Notification can be waived by a court order. This law has been ruled unconstitutional, so currently parents are not notified.

New Hampshire has no laws related to a minor's access to abortion.

New Jersey requires an unemancipated minor under 18 to wait at least 48 hours written notification of one parent. Notification can be waived by a court order. A court has ruled that this law in unconstitutional, so currently parents are not notified.

New Mexico requires that a minor under 18 have written consent of one parent. However, the N.M. Attorney General has ruled this unconstitutional, so currently no parental consent is required.

New York has no laws related to a minor's access to abortion.

North Carolina requires an unemancipated minor under 17 to have the written consent of one parent or one grandparent (with whom the minor has been living for at least six months). Consent can be waived by a court order.

North Dakota requires an unmarried minor under 18 to have the written consent of both parents. Consent can be waived by a court order.

Ohio requires an unemancipated minor under 18 to have written consent of one parent.Consent can be waived by a court order.

Oklahoma requires a minor to have parental consent and notification. Notification and consent can be waived by a court order.

Oregon has no laws related to a minor's access to abortion.

Pennsylvania requires an unemancipated minor under 18 to have informed consent of one parent. Consent can be waived by a court order.

Rhode Island requires an unemancipated, unmarried minor under 18 to have the consent of one parent. Consent can be waived by a court order.

South Carolina requires an unemancipated minor under 17 to have the informed written consent of one parent or grandparent. Consent can be waived by a court order.

South Dakota requires an unemancipated minor under 18 to wait at least 48 hours after a physician (or his agent) notifies one parent in writing. Notification can be waived by a court order.

Tennessee requires an unemancipated minor under 18 to have the written consent of one parent. Consent can be waived by a court order.

Texas requires an unemancipated minor under 18 to wait at least 48 hours after the physician has notified one parent, and the minor must have the notarized written consent of one parent. Notification and consent can be waived by a court order.

Utah requires an unemancipated minor under 18 to wait 24 hours after one parent has been notified. The minor must also have the informed written consent of one parent or guardian. Consent can be waived by a court order.

Vermont has no laws related to a minor's access to abortion.

Virginia law requires an unemancipated minor wait 24-hours after notifying an "authorized person" (which includes a parent, legal guardian, or another adult including a grandparent or adult sibling, with whom the minor resides and who has care and control of her. The minor must also have notarized written consent from the authorized person. Notification and consent can be waived by a court order.

Washington state has no laws related to a minor's access to abortion.

West Virginia requires an unemancipated minor under 18 who has not graduated from high school to wait at least 24 hours after notifying one parent. Notification can be waived by a court order or a physician.

Wisconsin requires an unemancipated minor under 18 to have the informed written consent of either one parent, a grandparent, aunt, uncle, or sibling who is at least 25 years old. Consent can be waived by a court order.

Wyoming requires an unmarried minor under 18 who is not in active military service or who not lived independently and apart from her parents for more than six months to wait at least 48 hours after notifying one parent and obtaining the written consent of one parent. Consent can be waived by a court order.

Appendix C: Discussion and Decision Checklist

For each topic, record your decision and some of the key reasons.

Housing options during pregnancy:
☐ Marry and live with spouse

☐ Live at home with parents

☐ Maternity Home

☐ Live with relative or friend.
Which person?
For how long?

☐ Live alone

Education Options:

☐ Finish at current school

☐ Go to night school

☐ Attend Special Needs School with the baby

☐ Home School or Tutor

☐Attend school online

Legal Issues:
☐ Contact Adoption Lawyer or Adoption Agency

☐ Learn Parental rights and obligations of birth mother

☐ Learn Parental rights and obligations of birth father

☐ Learn legal options and steps to take

Medical Issues:

☐ Put/keep minor child on parent's health plan

☐ Apply for Medicaid and WIC

☐ Check into health histories of parents

☐ Check into the fee schedule for prenatal care and delivery through local hospital

Options After Birth of Baby:

☐ Marriage

☐ Adoption

☐ Live with parents with baby

☐ Live with friends with baby

☐ Live alone/parent baby

☐ Parenting by close family member

☐ Maternity or Group home

Skill Building:
☐ Programs at Pregnancy Resource Center

☐ Prenatal Health

☐ Parenting skills

☐ Relationship skills

☐ Job Skills/ Career Plans

Appendix D: Resources

Parental Experiences

A Dad named Bill. *Daddy I'm Pregnant*. 1987. Multnomah Press.

A pastor shares his journal written during the time of his 14 year old daughter's pregnancy. He speaks about the choices that need to be made and shows the comfort and healing God provided.

Graham, Ruth and Dr. Sara Dormon, *I'm Pregnant...Now What?* 2004. Regal Books.

Ruth Graham, daughter of Billy Graham, and sister to Gigie, Ned, Anne and Franklin, tells the story of her 16-year-old daughter's pregnancy.

Wolff, Teresa L. *Mom, I'm Pregnant: Understanding and Guiding the Teenage Mother*. 1994. Sulzburger & Graham.

A guide to understanding the pregnant teen and strengthening the complex relationships with her family.

Schooler, Jayne. *Mom, Dad...I'm Pregnant.* 2004. NavPress

Spiritual Conflict

Anderson, Neil. *The Bondage Breaker*. 1990. Harvest House.

Armor for the spiritual battle against habitual sin, irrational feelings, and negative thoughts. Assurance that you can have victory and freedom in Christ.

Children's Books on God's Plan for Sex

Jacobson, Matt and Lisa. *The Amazing Beginning of You.* 2002. Zonderkids.
 A picture book exploring the development of a child in the womb.

Jones, S & B, C. Nystrom. *God's Design For Sex.* 1995. Navpress.
 Includes four books, (*The Story of Me* – ages 3 – 5, *Before I Was Born* – ages 5 – 8, *What's The Big Deal* – ages 8 – 11, and *Facing the Facts* – ages 11 – 14). This evangelical series presents age-appropriate discussion of God's plan for sex.

Organizations That Can Help

Bethany Christian Services
901 Eastern Avenue NE
PO Box 294
Grand Rapids, MI 49503-1295
1-800-238-4269
www.bethany.org
Provides pregnancy counseling, temporary foster care, and adoption services.

CareNet
44180 Riverside Parkway #200
Lansdowne, VA 20176
703-478-5661
1-800-395-HELP (4357)
www.care-net.org
National network of pregnancy centers providing free pregnancy tests, medical, and professional services.

Heartbeat International
665 E. Dublin-Granville Rd #440
Columbus, OH 43229-3245
1-800-395-HELP (4357)

www.heartbeatinternational.org
A network of crisis pregnancy centers and maternity homes.

Liberty Godparent's Home
P.O. Box 4199
Lynchburg, VA 24502
1-800-542-4453
www.godparent.org
Maternity home and other resources for pregnant women.

Nurturing Network
www.nurturingnetwork.org
Offers practical support to college and working women with unplanned pregnancies.

Toll-Free Numbers/Hotlines

American Pregnancy Helpline
1-888-467-8466
www.thehelpline.org

National Life Center
1-800-848-LOVE (5683)
Pregnancy Hotline

OptionLine
1-800-395-HELP (4357)

Sharing Your Story

Thank you for picking up "How To Survive Your Teen's Pregnancy"! We hope it has been very valuable to you. As time passes and the pain and emotions settle a little, would you mind sharing a bit of your story with us?

Would you tell us ...
The major feelings you wanted help with when you began reading this book?

The main problems you were facing?

Were these issues adequately addressed in the book?

Do you feel you received healing with these issues?

In what areas do you still need help?

Thank you for helping us improve this book! Please email your comments to info@chalfonthouse.com or mail them to Chalfont House, PO Box 84, Dumfries, VA 22026. May God bless you!